RUSSIA

SSIYSK

BATUMI

5. JULY24-23

TBLISI

GEORGIA

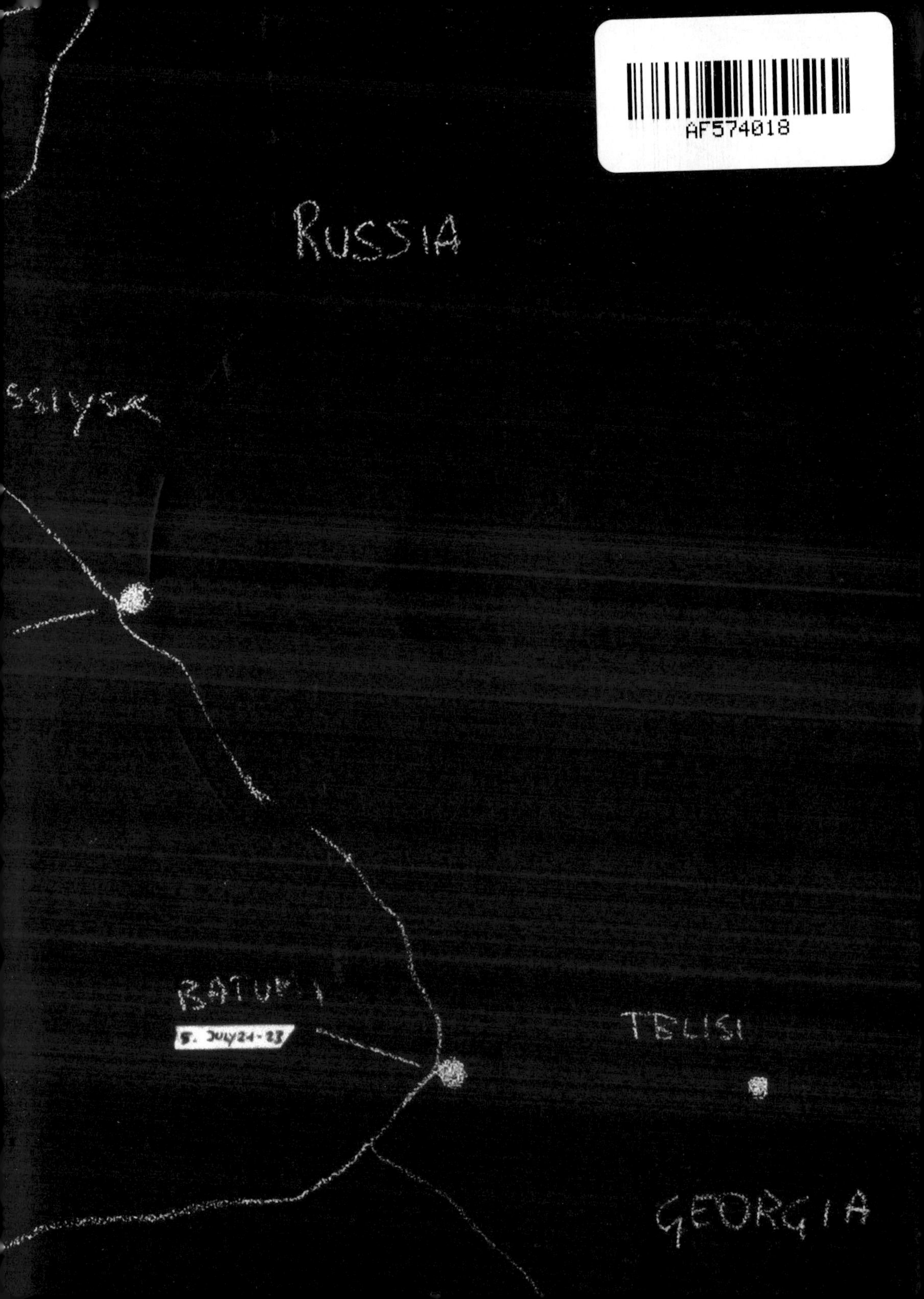

ZAGZIG series
directed by
Philippe Langlois & Frank Smith

in the same series

Laurie Anderson: *Nothing in my Pockets*
Jonas Mekas: *To Petrarca*
Lee Ranaldo & Leah Singer: *Water Days*
Ryoji Ikeda: *Dataphonics*
Gisèle Vienne, Dennis Cooper, Peter Rehberg: *Jerk // Through their tears*
Chloé: *Chasser Croiser—The Surreal and its echo*

1 Cité Riverin
75010 Paris
France
www.disvoir.com
ISBN 978-2-914563-66-6

The sound piece *Medea*
free CD n°ZagZig/07/1

Translated by Paul Buck & Catherine Petit
Design: Pascale Willi
Digital Post production: Metamorphosis

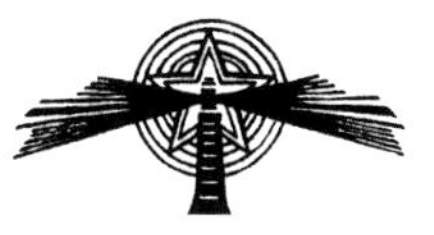

MEDEA

COLLECTION FROM THE BLACK SEA

Pictures: Stephan Crasneanscki
Text: Arthur Larrue

Sound piece: Soundwalk Collective
Stephan Crasneanscki
Dug Winningham
Simone Merli
Kamran Sadeghi
Jake Harper

Music Advisor: Jean-Yves Leloup

Captain: Romain Servat

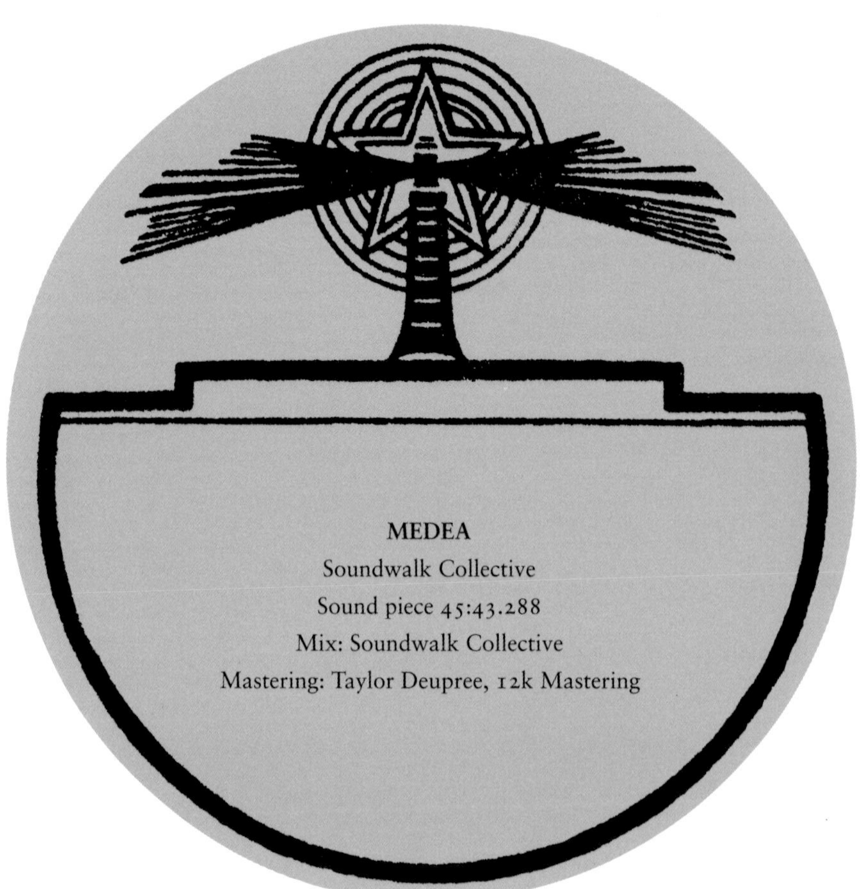
MEDEA
Soundwalk Collective
Sound piece 45:43.288
Mix: Soundwalk Collective
Mastering: Taylor Deupree, 12k Mastering

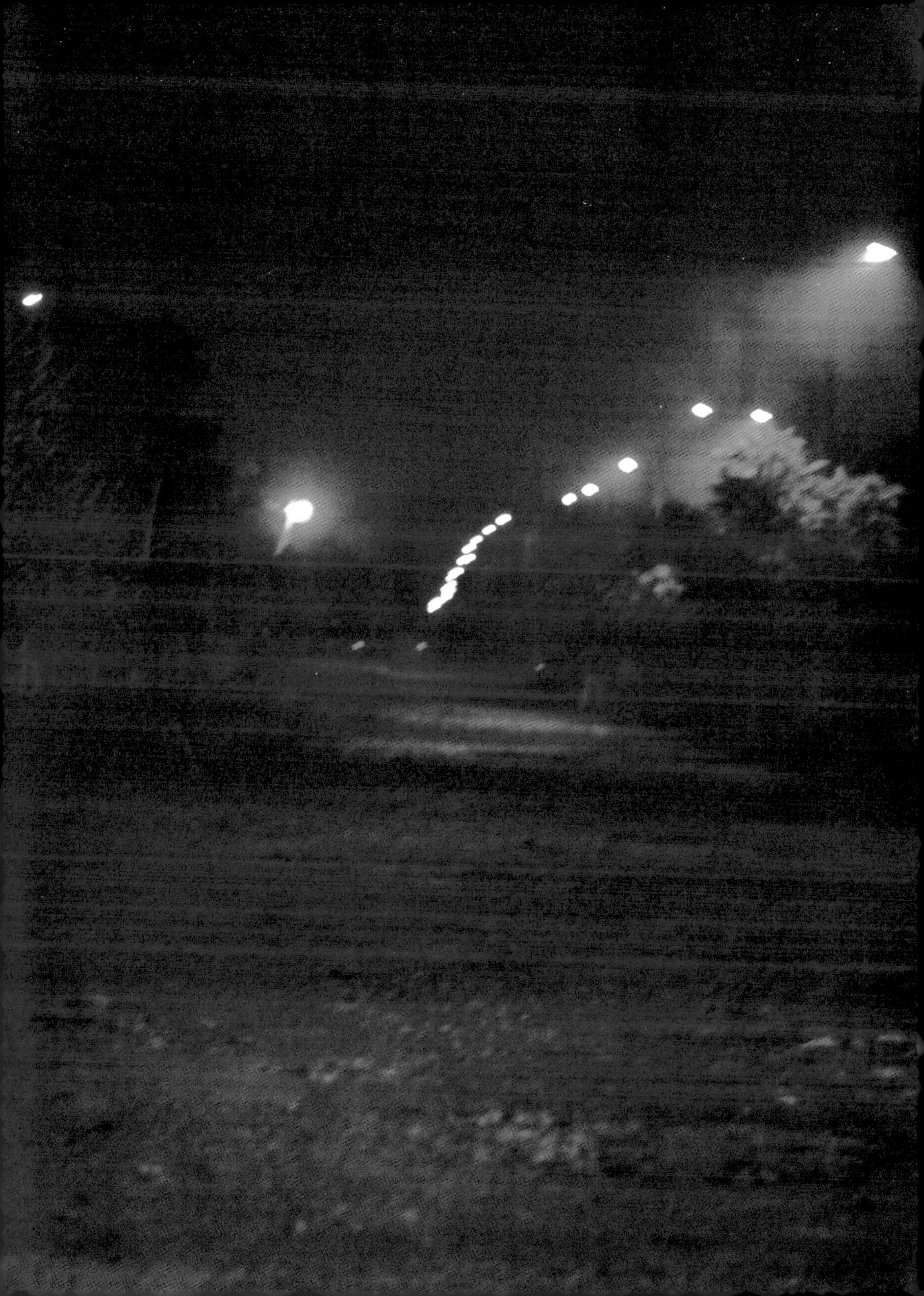

The Black Sea is like any other sea in the world, it repeats the same things many times with waves always beginning again, and yet no one seems to understand it, no one appears to listen to it even.

Stephan Crasneanscki has gathered around him in the Soundwalk Collective, whose founder he is, a team of four sound artists: Kamran Sadeghi, Simone Merli, Jake Harper and Dug Winningham. They climb aboard a twenty-eight meter long schooner and travel for two months along the shore of the Black Sea, from Istanbul to Burgas, through seven countries, coasting. They will etch grooves in that inhabited silence, they will record the sonic squeaks, sailors' dialogues, the moans of the rigging.... all the things that will compose their journey when one closes one's eyes.

My name is Arthur Larrue, I shall be with them, I am going to write what could be a Journal of the Black Sea if Medea doesn't become the tutelary figure of that sound journey. For Stephan is convinced that if that sea possesses a language of its own, it is to the magician Medea that the meaning should be asked.

We are in Istanbul, 28 52' 73 E, the air is extremely peppery.
Tomorrow I shall talk about yesterday.

Soundwalk played *Ulysse Syndrome* at the Haymatlos Club.

It was the revelation of all that which one usually doesn't listen to or simply half-listens to, and immediately forgets.

How many sounds escape us? Aren't they, for all that, one of the primordial aspects of our environment? During the performance, those sounds appeared as an oppor-tunity for a reading of ourselves and if we had been able to, we would have rolled our eyes over to see our souls dancing inside our heads.

We slept there where we had fallen, we had been drinking, it had been a beautiful party. To feel more at ease, the Turkish girls had taken off their shoes and danced bare feet. We had done the same, it was important we felt, for the last time, a ground that didn't pitch. We were apprehensive about being tossed around on the water for the two months our crossing would last...

—

The Bosphorus is a water corridor bordered by hills. We are recording the muezzins' songs that echo one another across the banks. A thousand tankers begin their rounds and disturb the waters, they draw ten meters and have stems dented like the foreheads of pachyderms. On each summit in Turkey the national flag flies proudly, for Turkish people like to remind us that we are in their country. The minarets are needles, the houses hang on the slopes, the vegetation is scrub, and the rocks black.

In the distance is the horizon of the Black Sea, flatter and more empty as we emerge from a narrow corridor. The mystery that stretches in front of us is perhaps that darkness of the Black Sea – a vast abyss coming out of a Bosphorus that, compared to it, is as thin as a lizard's tongue. Our sailing boat has taken shelter in the little cove of Poyraz.

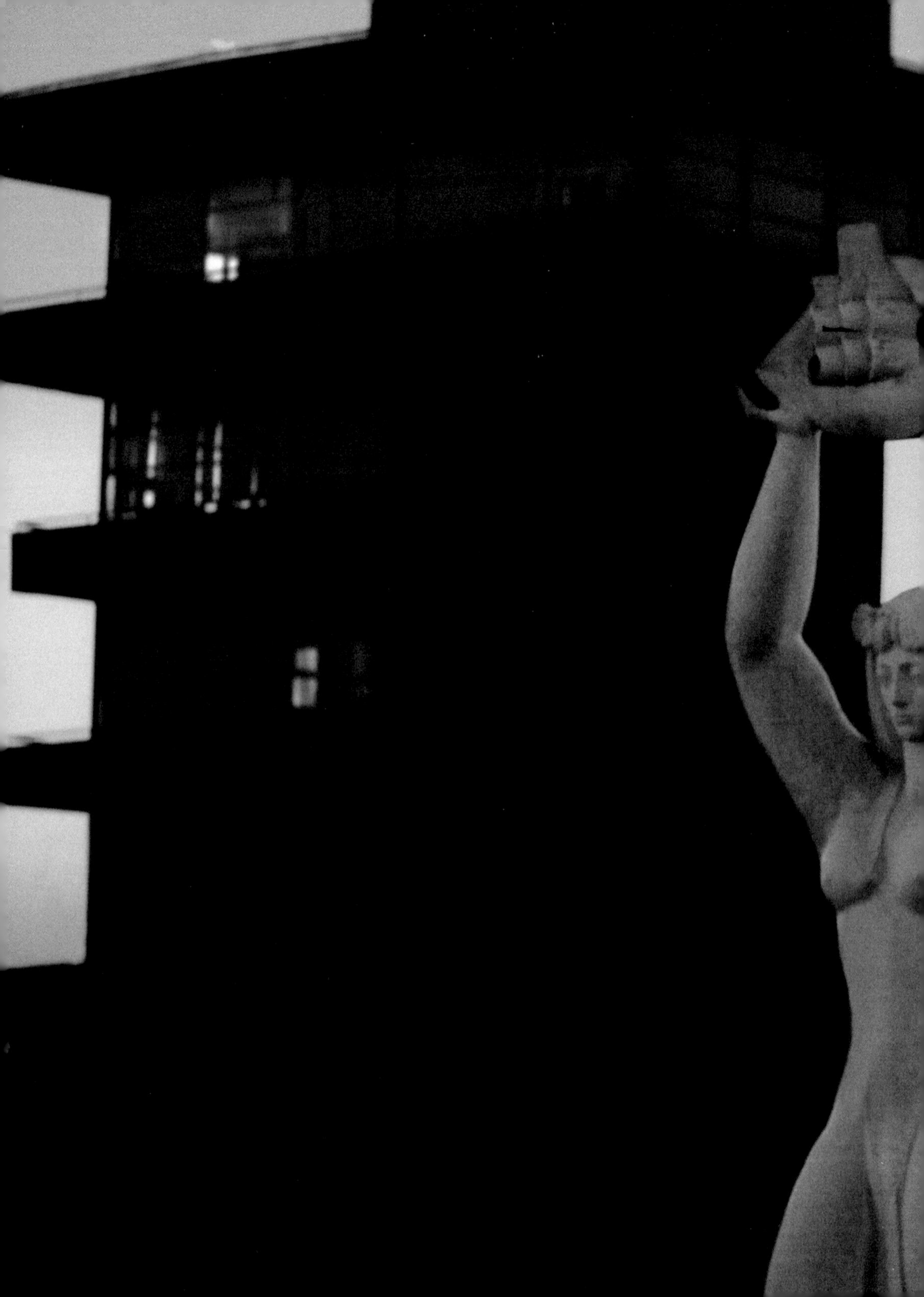

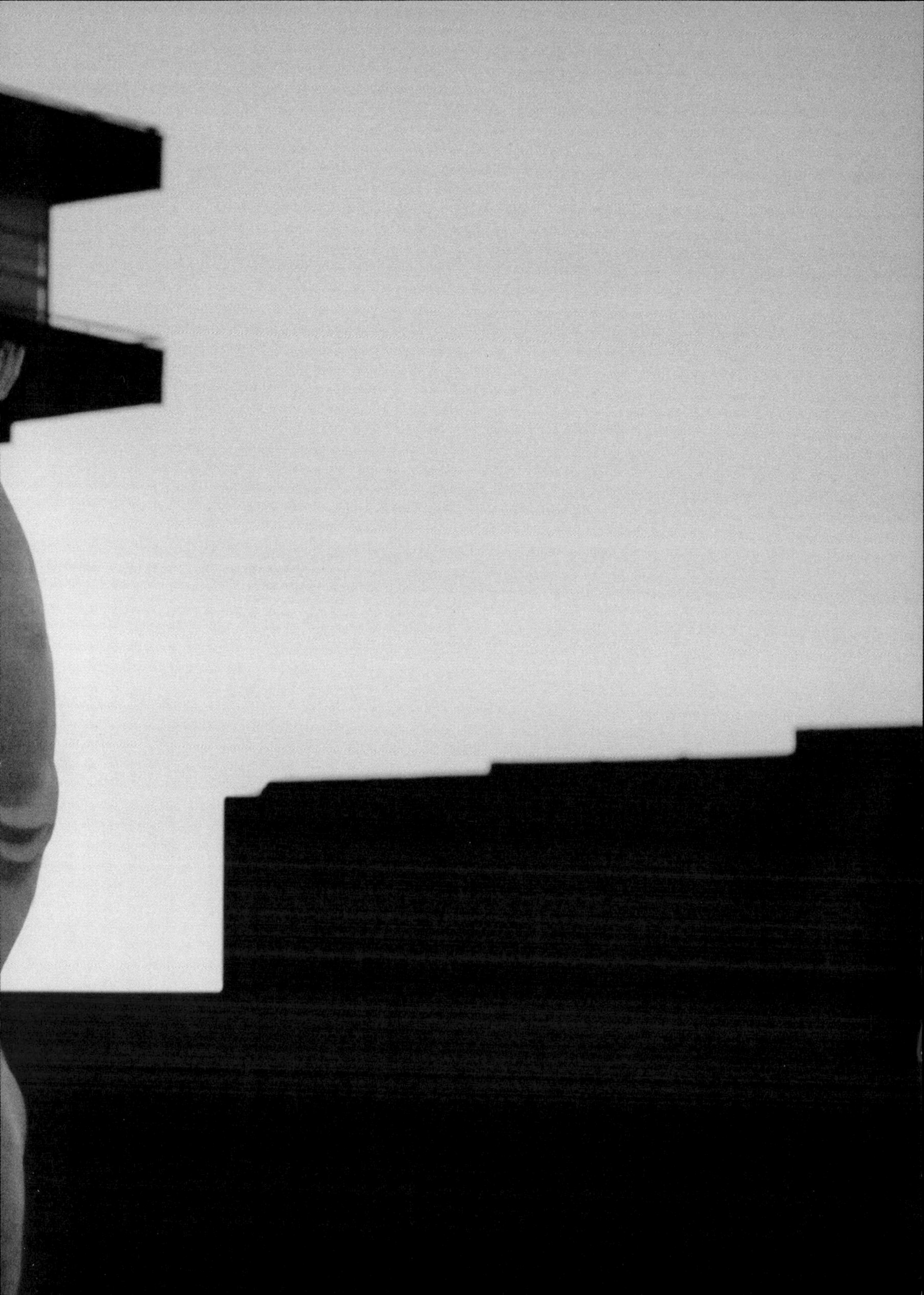

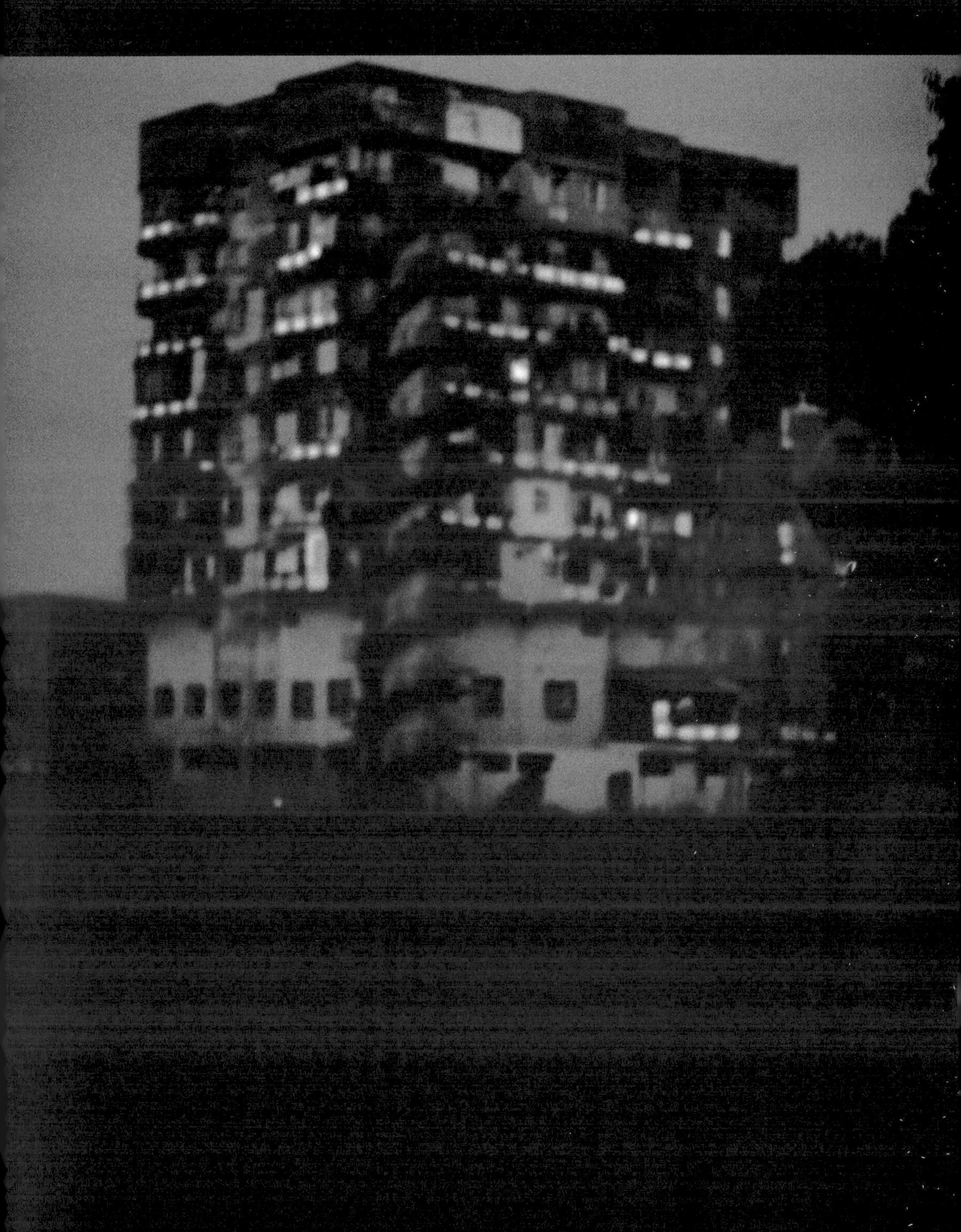

29 07.708' E

We are looking at the coast and its numerous bathers with apprehension, from afar, from our sound lab that has become a republic of men fishing for sounds. For while we live happily on water, we are afraid of the land.

Zonguldak 31 47.127' E
Kastamonu 33 46.20' E

To say that we are moving on the Black Sea is a relative truth. Soundwalk progresses on what should be seen as a vast flat surface on which radio waves travel freely. A matrix. There is no solitude. We see no one, however we pick up insignificant, serious, furtive messages from thousands of men and women whose paths cross or move away. We record the totality of those words and we classify them. Those waves have a body, they display themselves in colourful curves on our computer screens, and we recompose them with sophisticated software. We will make a symphony out of them, which will also be a sound anthropology.

Yakakent 35 30.126' E

There is this quotation by Kazimir Malevitch: "Whose mission is it to acknowledge the living moves through invisible and immaterial ways, those ways – his waves – are perhaps the essential in him.

Our scanners catch curious words

– Ben gelyorum!

(creaking)

– Любовь моя!... птичка моя!

– femeile nu sunt pe ap_.

(creaking)

The waves speak all languages.
We take samples, then we fragment them.

A tapestry should be imagined to understand what we are doing as we superimpose several sound layers aimed at creating a landscape with no image, one that only exists through suggestions and whispers.

Tire Bolu N41 O'41

The waves are the components of an invisible world one has to go into.
We haven't caught a single fish since our departure.

—

143.6 MHz. We had a strange encounter. We were having lunch, Simone had connected the mobile scanner AR8200 just in case, because one never knows who can suddenly speak from any point in the sea. We had set four other more powerful scanners but it's not them that picked up the surprise encounter. They were searching between 156 MHz and 158 MHz on the frequencies reserved for marine traffic: they were on the wrong track. A little machine with a flexible radio aerial one meter five long, covering eight miles, it was placed between a dish of olives stuffed with peppers and a plate with yoghurt with herbs; it was our backup scanner. Plugged into a tape recorder (a kind of ancient grey walkman with a digital screen), it was searching for an "inhabited" frequency without really believing in it,

The numbers filed past, from thousandths to hundredths, then on 143.6 MHz, we heard the sound of a Turkish flute, beautiful like the very old mechanism of a badly oiled door: a Zourna.

Theological questions are frequent on the radio waves where we are, flutes are rare, often they ask the meaning of such and such sura from the Koran. Ghosts' voices were answering in serious tones, it was a heaven-sent flute. An old Turkish fisherman, for sure. He was playing for the anchovies he had caught, or the anchovies he was going to catch. To attract them?

We imagined him sitting on a net, with a thick moustache, his eyes washed by the sea. He played for just over three minutes. We didn't see his caique, or his face. He was "the Turkish fisherman of 143.6 MHz".

Trabzon E39 44’21

Trabzon is a town on the slope of a mountain, with cranes and cargo ships, small narrow streets where one can find barbers, pastry dripping with honey and a strange fizzy carrot juice called sira. Stephan and Simone left for the mountains in search of some singers who still remembered the ancestral songs of the Black Sea. It was more than three hours on the road, the car almost toppled into the ravine, the gears screeching. On their return, they talked about men drunk on tea and tobacco, gathered around a copper stove, playing dominos with small ivory rectangles on which were etched clover and numbers. While the women worked, the men let time slip by. And when the little troupe of tea drinkers with deep and black wrinkles were stirred to play and sing, they told me how they were moved to tears. The traditional Turkish violin has three positions and screeched even more than our 143.6 MHz. Up there, it was misty, the grass was lush and it was cold.

—

Our scanners recorded the first Georgian words, we were approaching Batumi. It’s a language that comes from the back of the throat, it is pronounced with accents that sing. Its writing is very beautiful, it has something archaic and voluptuous about it: საქართველო means Georgia.

Batumi E41 38.62

The Golden Fleece was kept in Batumi. Having just arrived there, we found the beautiful Medea. It occurred in a bar that had just opened, a former chemist. The owner was wearing a needle moustache and didn’t want to speak Russian because of the war. We danced and explained our sonic journey. There was a very pretty girl in a polka dot dress whom we all fell in love with. At times she escaped on a red bicycle and then came back a few minutes later. When I left, she was reading Hemingway’s Farewell to Arms in a corner. It was past four in the morning, she undoubtedly has a sense of the spectacle about her!

"You are Medea in a polka dot dress, you have bewitched us all and your alphabet casts magic spells, and your edition is an old book of potions and finally it is very dubious to occupy oneself with literature at that hour of the morning."

—

With Georgian musicians, we learn the meaning of the word concession:
– Arthur, ask them to take turns singing...
– They don't want to, their traditional songs are written for three singers.
– They cannot make exceptions?
– They say tradition has no exception or else it's no tradition.
– Well, at least make sure there are sailors' songs.
– They say Georgian people are not sailors but mountain people.
– But our project is about the Black Sea!
– They say they look at the Black Sea from the mountain but fishing bores them They say the tambourine won't.....
– Okay, tell them to do what they want!
– That's exactly what they intended to do!

—

In Georgian, the name of the president Dimitri Saakachvili is written like this: საქართველო ს პრეზიდენტი . He is a man with two heads for he seems to be a past master in the art of dissimulation. He has bearing but an anxious soul, a forced smile, a youthfulness in his gestures, but the greyish temples of a man grown old through power. He rules his little piece of Caucasus like an American – he is half-American – and it appears as out of place in the surrounding mountains. His entourage is made up of pretty girls in silk, ribbons, curls and pearls. They say he is a womaniser. Perhaps he is simply a president, that job is not entirely like any other. One has countless privileges. Among them, to be surrounded day and night by forty or so beefy blokes dressed in black.

Soundwalk played for him in the rather bizarre setting of a cocktail party, on the top floor of a luxury hotel. The president asked formal and hasty questions, Stephan wanted to get him interested. It's not easy to impress a president, so one lies a little...

– What type of music do you play?
– Sound journeys...
– Where do you come from?
– New York.
– How did you arrive in Batumi?
– By boat.
– By boat! From New York? To Batumi?
– Yes, Mr President.
– How long did it take?
– Three months, Mr President.
– ...

The president left, still puzzled.
During the concert, three projectors showed waves moving, the foam at times resembling curls of smoke, at other times Rorschach ink blots tests[1].

One sees in them what one wants to see.

—

(Recording of a dialogue from our schooner's radio.)

– Frequency 12, are you leaving the harbour? Because I can see you going...
– Yes, we are lifting anchor. Over.
The port authority of Batumi's harbour must have been quite sad to mumble like that... We left behind us a long grey wake, I think it took quite a while to disappear.
We should have as many lives as there are countries.

—

1. NDE The Rorschach test or test of ink blots consists of a series of symmetrical spots that are offered for free interpretation by the subject whose responses presents matter for his personality to be studied.

Stephan said he had invited Medea on board our sound lab. Medea will be with us from Batumi to Poti. She was not wearing her polka dot dress but a backless dress with purple flowers that swelled in the wind like a balloon. That dress could have flown away or unveiled bits of flesh. We were all aware of the slightest movement on her part. Her man was with her, he was called Gueorgui and he was having a nap. When Medea went for a swim, he used her dress to protect his face from the sun and snooze a little more. We imagined the happiness of being under her spell like that.

—

<u>Poti E41 39'30</u>

Poti was the place where Medea left on the Argos. It is where she left her country for ever, it's also where the Ottoman Empire traded slaves from the East. Today huge tankers load oil there. The town is gradually falling to rust and shows signs of age; there reigns that sad and genuine atmosphere of Soviet towns where the humanity of the residents is brought out more, made more salient because of adversity.

A statue of the magician guards the harbour, holding above her head the boat of her lover Jason. It is our boat, in a way, that she salutes, with her cold eyes and her skin the colour of chalk. We are sailing again today: two days without sight of land, for we must avoid the Abkhazie and its pirates.

<u>Off the coast of Vardane E45 39.67</u>

The radio waves are increasingly rare sixty miles from the coast. The scanners only pick up a mysterious woman's voice chanting Russian numbers, interrupted and eaten by cracklings, at the limit of intelligibility, as if gnawed. Something sensual passed through however.

Один два три восемь *(crackling)* десять пятого (*crackling)* кстати…

What does that mean?

And if it didn't mean anything at all?

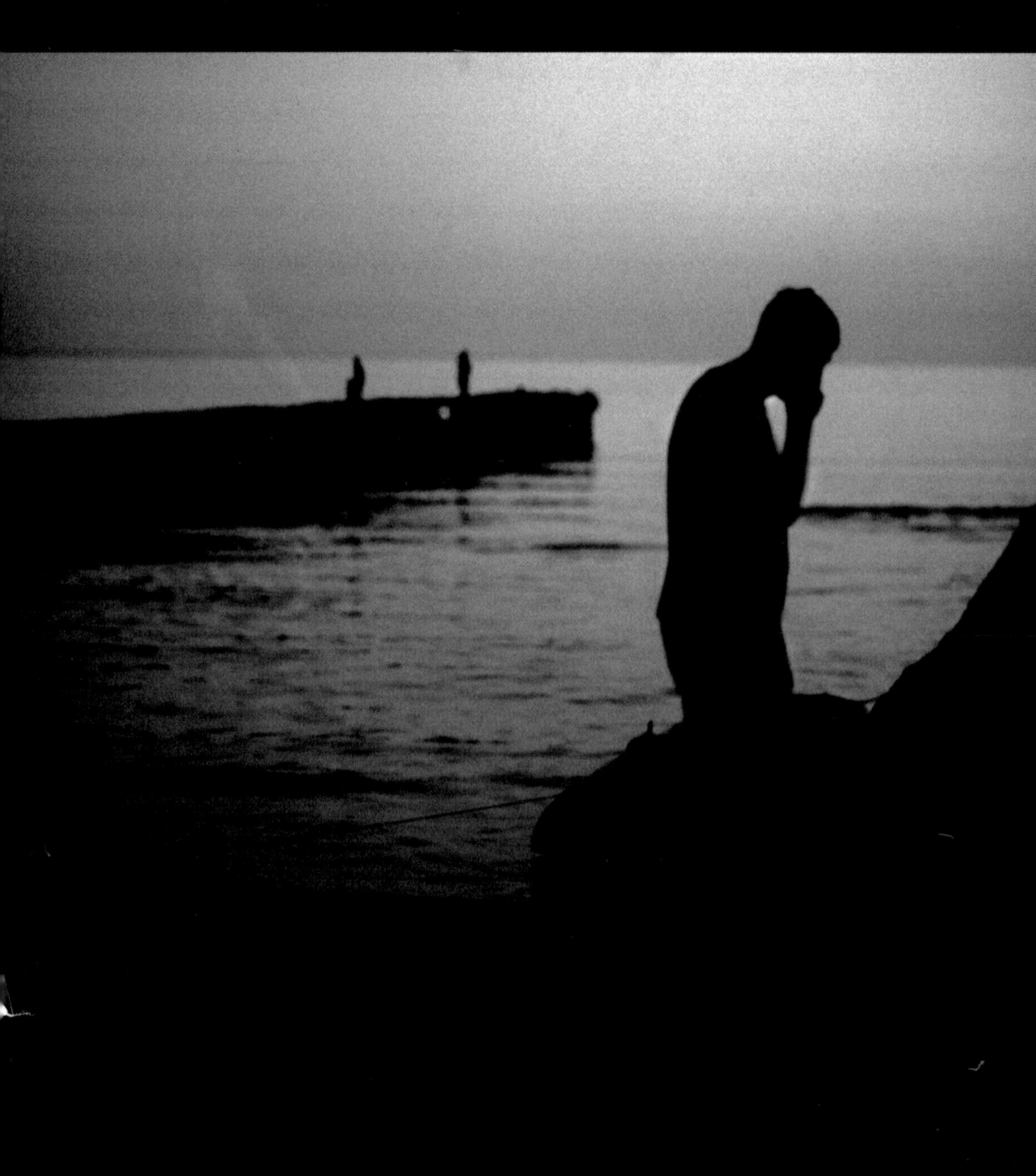

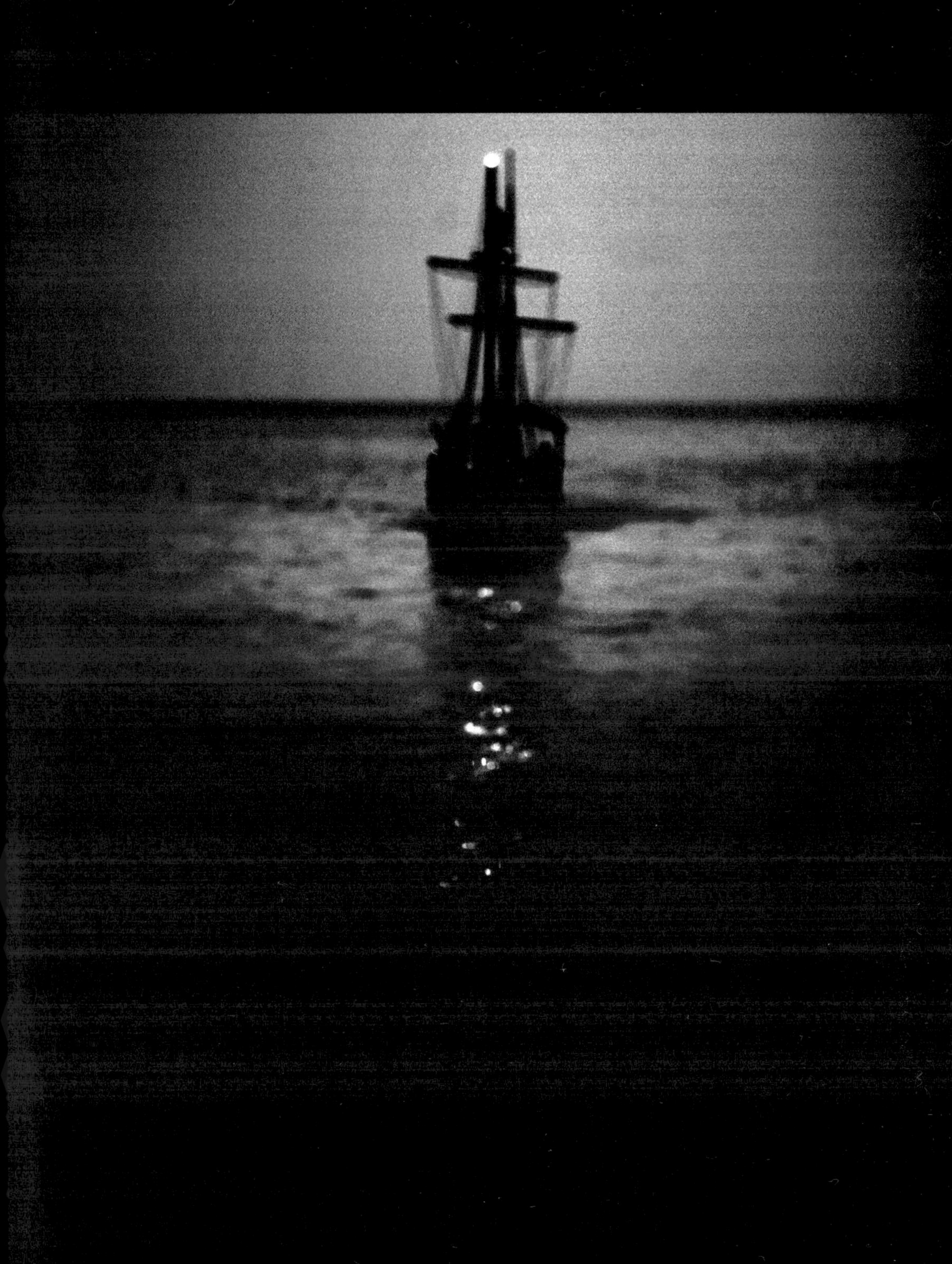

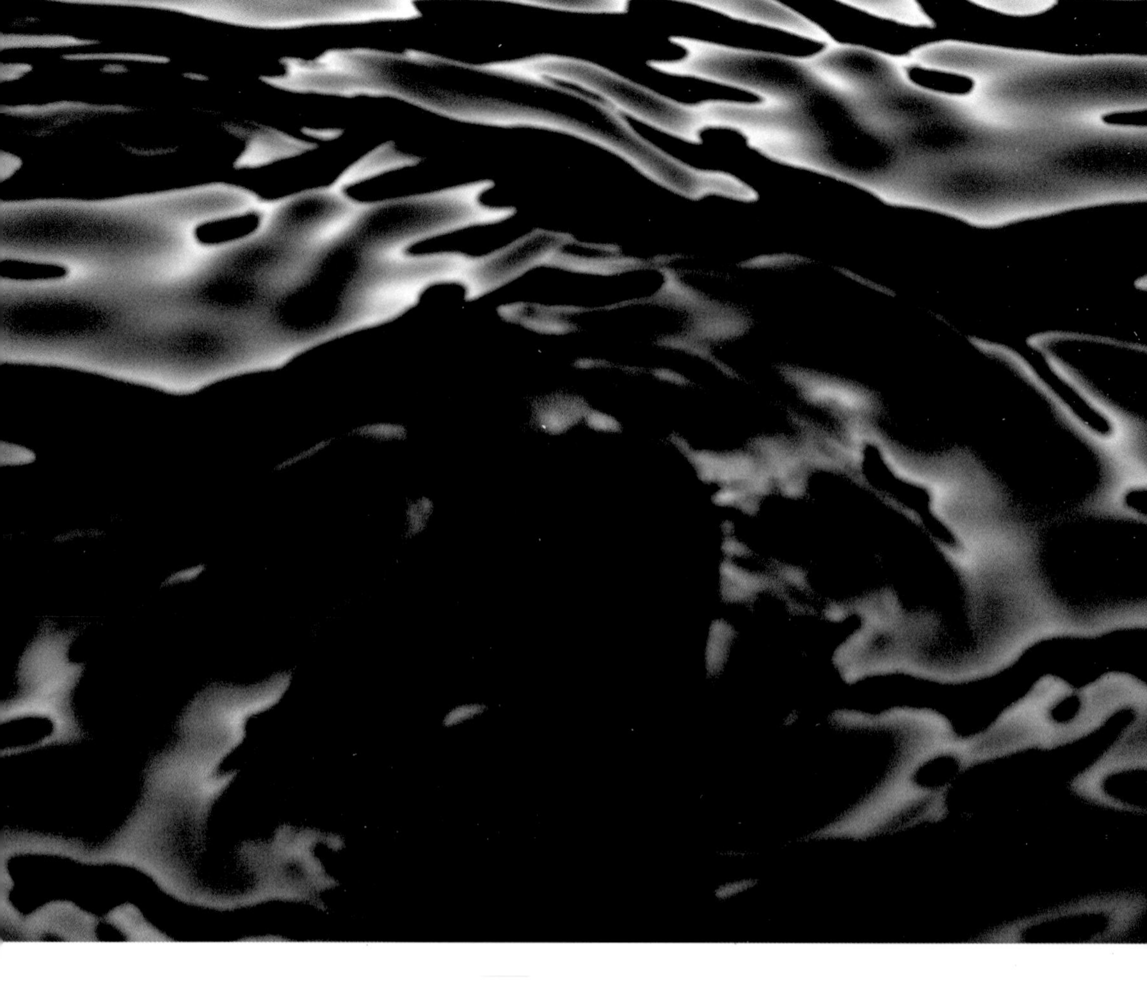

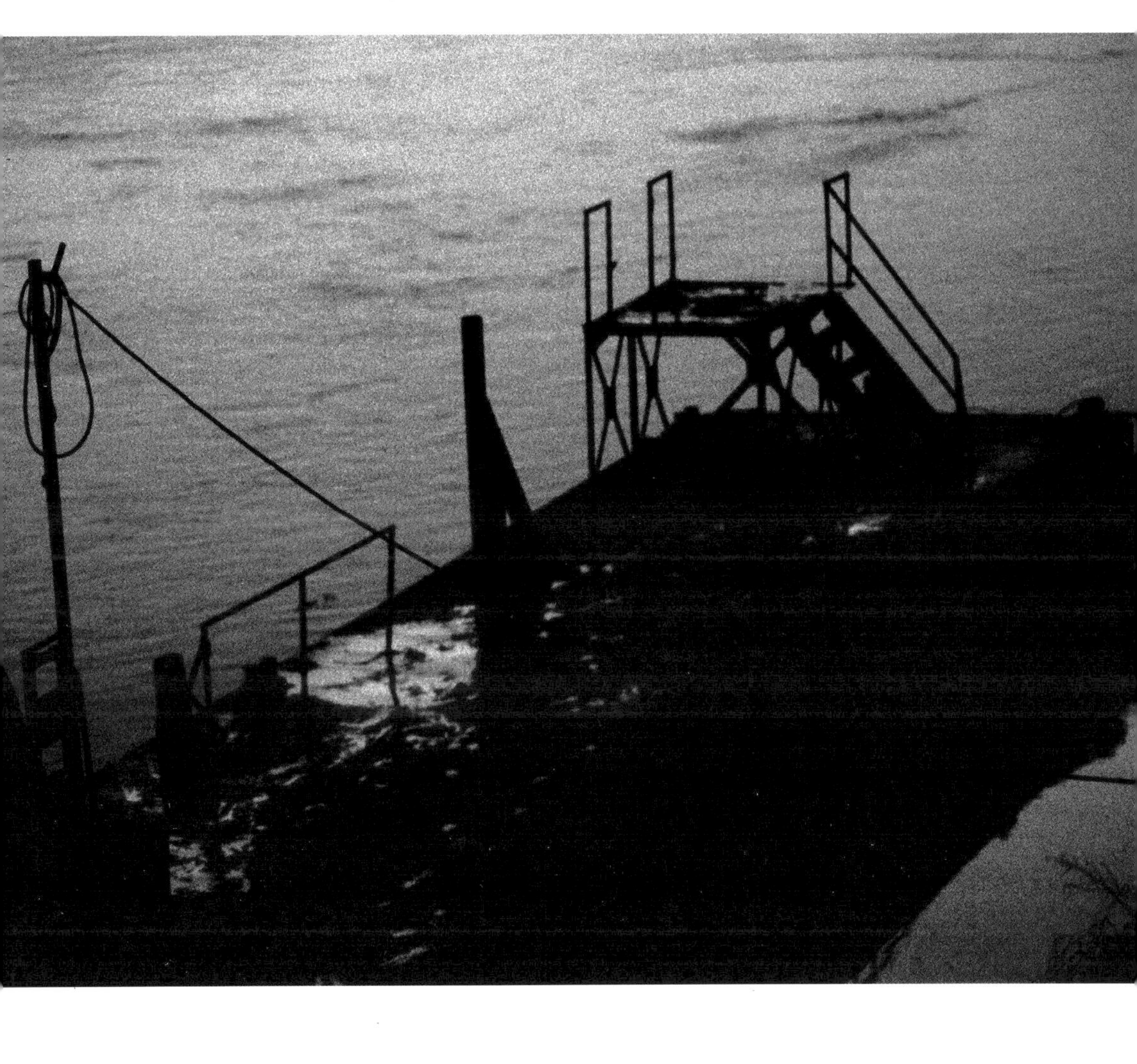

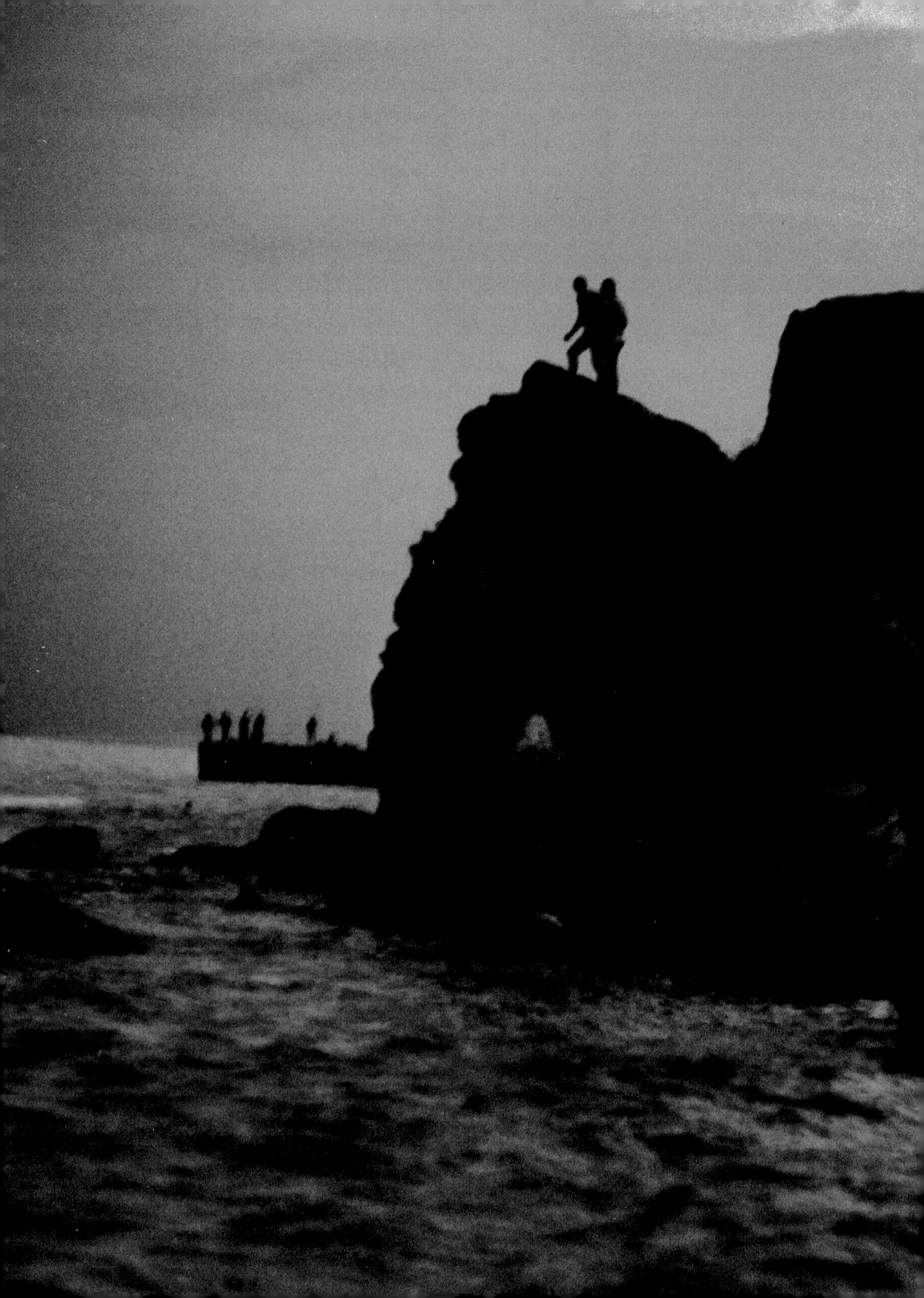

Open sea E47 36.98

It is important to become introspective, to cease all dispersion. Each member of our
sonic republic has felt the opportunity for solitude that the open sea offers.
We talked little, perhaps we had said it all, or perhaps it was too much to say
something? All became vanity. I found this pleasing sentence in the manual of
the AR 8600 handheld scanner: "*As never earth to a gaz pipe*". It made me dream.
Who would think of connecting a scanner to a gas pipeline? That first day
in the open sea was a condensed life, each minute like a grain of sand.
The voice of the Russian woman was still chanting
Один два три восемь (*crackling*) десять пятого (*crackling*) кстати...

—

We are led, at the mercy of the whims of the sea and the wind;
Soundwalk has placed microphones at water level to record the waves,
they are hung from the mast to pick up the sound of the rigging.
We had to whisper – all day long it was like that – "listening".

– Romain, captain, why not hoist the sails more to go faster?
– Because the wind is getting stronger, the sea rears, the sky is turning blind,
and I don't want to break the masts.
– Does that mean there's going to be a storm?
– Yes!

—

Storm E46 38.33

The radio hadn't forecast anything alarming. The Russian weather report just
warned us that we would be gently pushed by the wind. We were not going to cross
any shipping lanes, cargo or tankers: we would be alone for twenty-four hours.
It came across with the night, we could only see darkness around and waves
becoming white against the hull. We could no longer stand up.

I was the first to throw up and a few others followed, squatting, emptying our guts while the boat took a nosedive. It was going up and down, it made us sick. We had to fill up on bread, drink nothing and lie flat. The crockery went flying, we hit the walls. There was nothing around us except for a dense darkness that was moving like a kind of furious oil, bent on swallowing us whole. As for Stephan, he was smiling broadly, he didn't suffer from seasickness and felt triumphant to see us like that, broken.
We had to record the lightning and the horrible cracking of the wood.
For that, we had to screw Kamran's microphone (the one that resembles
a big cat) to big red and green claws then to tape them to the deck,
and to add ropes...

I was green like a Van Dongen portrait. I don't want to remember, so I'm going to narrate the end: it came with the land. As soon as Crimea was in sight, the sea calmed. It was unbelievable, the grey mountains, half-sketched, lost in the morning mist, caught in doubt.

– Look, there's land!

– No, it's clouds...

– It's land, I tell you! Crimea! Ukraine! Yalta!

– If what you say is true, then Medea's wrath has abated...

Yalta N44 28'83

Здорова ребята!... Бум!... бум зук зук бам...
We reached Yalta in the morning, all was fluorescent: the people and the noise. We were half dead and unsocial after two days and nights at sea. The calm after the storm. We saw the pink beaches, the crowds, the big inflatables, the costumes, and music spitting. We wanted to leave but had to stay. Yalta has pretty streets lined with trees, crumbling houses, rooms to rent, stories and History: Chekhov, Stalin... Old people have gold teeth, young women are the most beautiful in the world, boys roll up their T-shirts to let their stomachs breathe, or walk around in their underwear. Couples are made of princesses and frogs.

We were caught by surprise, we were coming from another world.
Jake left for an expedition to the Russian-Ukrainian border with the AR 2600 handheld scanner.

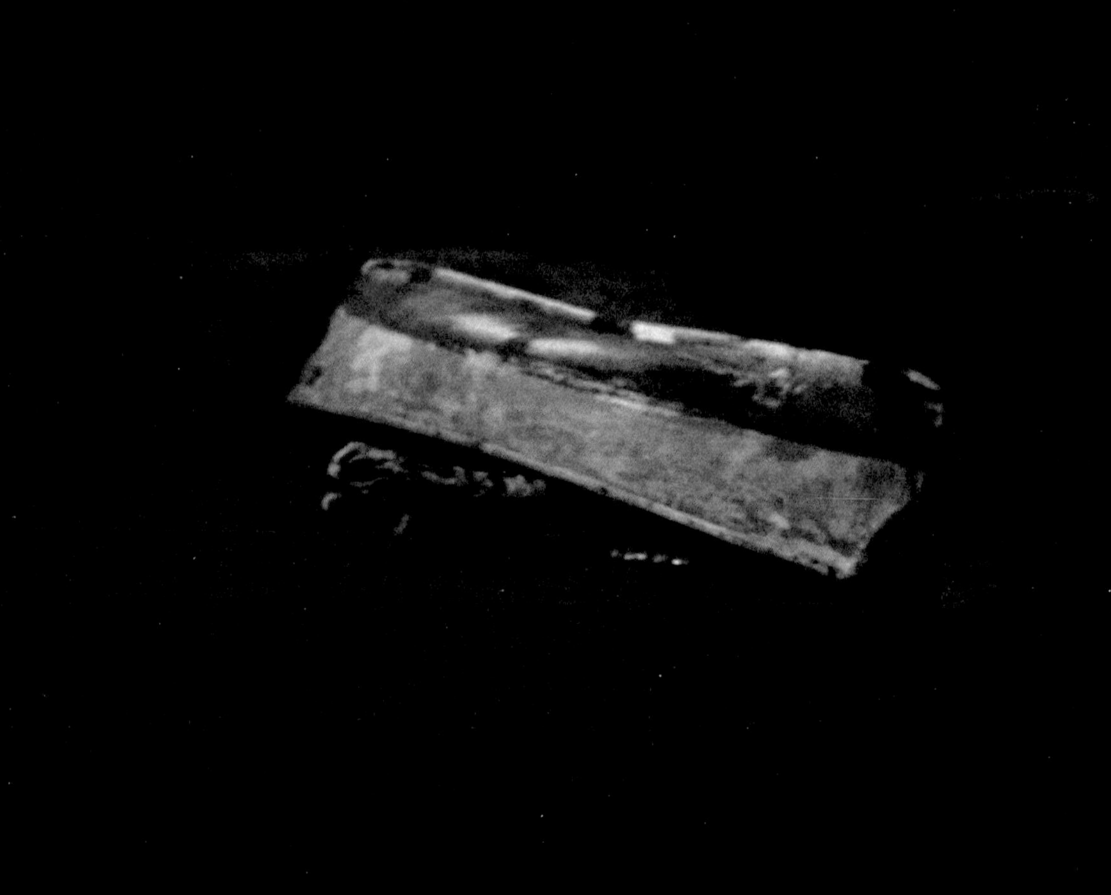

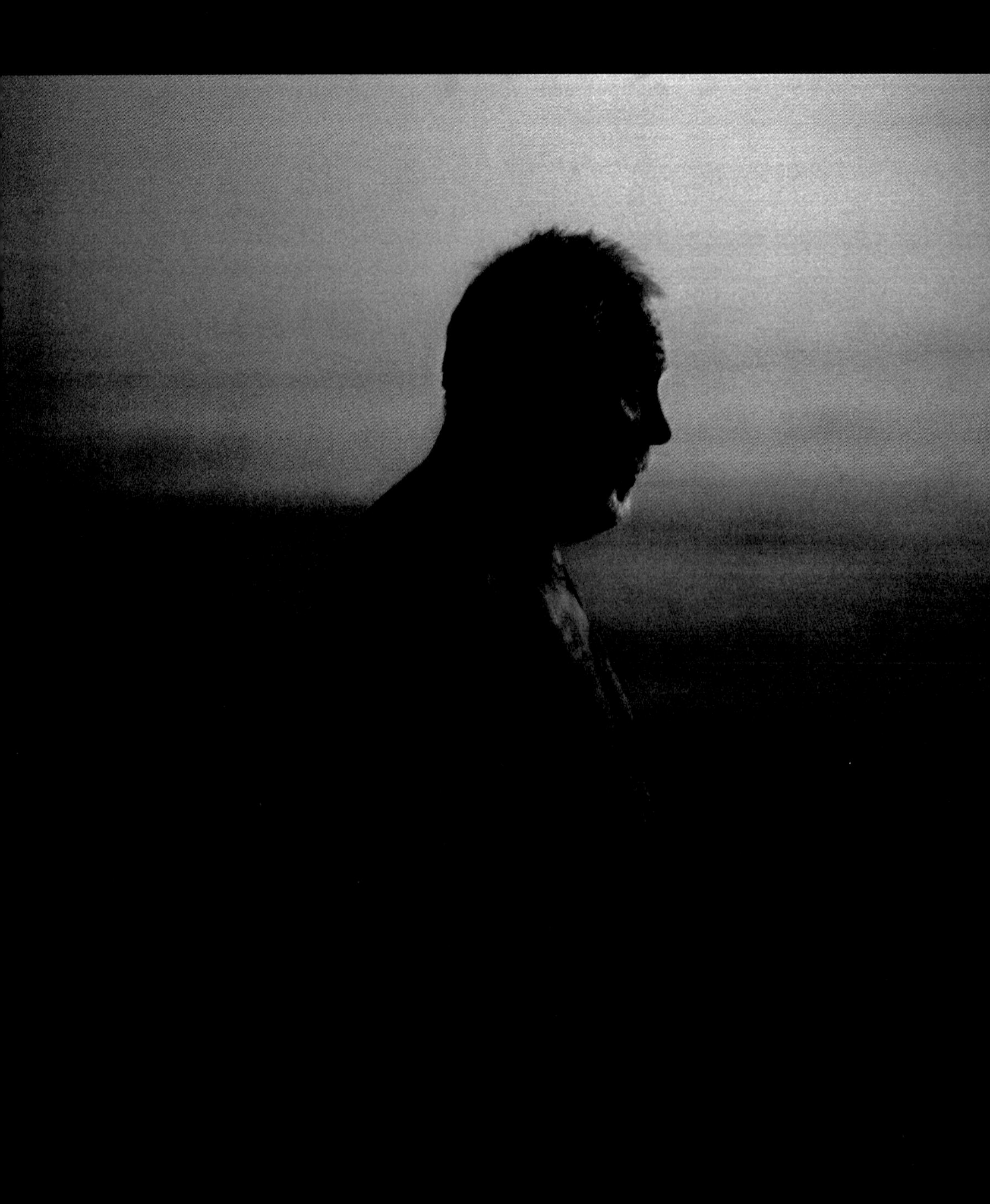

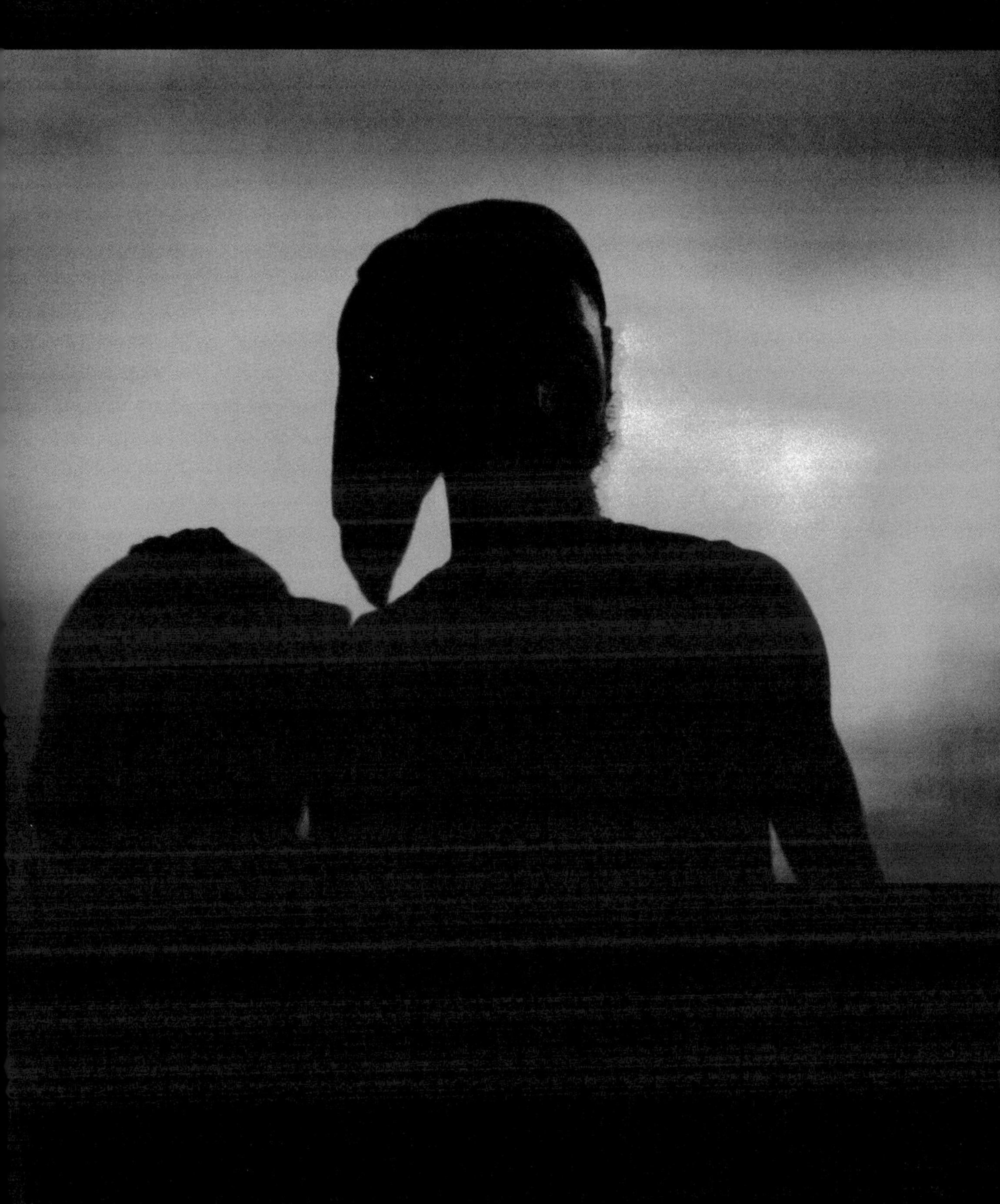

We need Russian voices, someone said. He must have taken
refuge in a hotel room, sleeping on the audio cables.
Девушкие!... Девушкие!... Девушкие!...
The voices we picked up in the open sea cannot be traced, remained unknown.
One would need to speak all the languages and live
as many times as there are countries...
Здорова ребята!... Бум!... бум зук зук бам...

Balaklava E33 34'96

The Black Sea is not black, but has white spots.
Billions of jellyfish are floating, they don't sting, they have only a jelly cap and no
purple filament on their extremities. When we go for a swim, we disturb them. The
noise from Yalta has faded away, dwellings have become rare, the coast sometimes
unveils big architectural oddities: sanatoriums in the shape of UFOs, blocks of
apartments with pastel blue balconies, villas like Bavarian castles.
Those constructions are isolated, on the hillsides, on a green and beige background.
From the sea, one contemplates them like works of art. There are also the illegal
campsites of the hippies from the East, they move about on overloaded boats, grill
their fish. Nature is superb, it still belongs to the people, nothing fancy or tacky. We
were looking at all those things, the wind didn't blow at all,
we moved with the engine. Stephan had his magic ears working though.
– I can hear crickets!
– It's the engine, Stephan!
– No, there are crickets.
– How on earth can you hear crickets when the engine...
– I said crickets. Wanna bet?

When we stopped the engine to check his intuition, we heard a thunder of crickets:
twenty-five decibels times thousands, to be precise, since an isolated
migrating cricket (*Schitocerca gregaria*) alone produces twenty-five decibels!

Stephan is the kind of magician to own a cicada in a cage to listen to it singing its laments, like an ancient aesthete described by Theocritus.

–

Sébastopol E33 31'67
Evpatoria N45 18'67
Ordjonikidze N45 00'86.1

We are looking for the Tartars of Crimea.
– I'm a Tartar from Crimea.
– What's your name?
– Youssouf.
– Where are the other Tartars from Crimea, Youssouf?
– In Central Asia.
– Then why are they "from Crimea"?
– Because Stalin had them all deported there!
He replaced them with Russian bear hunters.
Stalin was a maker of seas, lands and peoples.
The most destructive creator of History.
– Therefore, if we look for Russian fishermen songs on the Black Sea…
– They will sing you the taiga, the tundra, the Ural….
– Did the Tartars come back here?
– Yes, a little. But they have no school, no books, only their memory.
– What about their music?
– I know a mother and son.

The Tartar played the clarinet and his mother sang with an ice-cold, fragile voice. Her vocal cords must have been thin like filaments in tungsten, they trembled dangerously. "*It's because I haven't eaten for sixteen hours, the Ramadan…*" Her son, on the contrary, blew as much as he could into his clarinet, turning redder than his Crimean Tartar's skin.

Tchernomorsk N45 11'23.5

DIn that little cove, music blared at 105 decibels.
A little illuminated train went along the shore.
Recipe for a "White Russian":
1/3 white vodka
20 grams of black Kailua
50 grams of cream
3 ice cubes
Shake five times in a shaker and resume our sound quest elsewhere.
We didn't find any sound for Medea and the Black Sea,
only Russians on holiday talking about the White Sea.

—

Odessa E30 44'98.7

We reached Odessa at nightfall. Our whole republic was at the bow,
the boat in the exact axis of the setting sun. We felt we were going to meet it,
pass with it into the other hemisphere, find ourselves in China in one single go,
like one turns a page or flips a dish. Hop!
We could also have planted the masts in the sun, become stars ourselves,
we could have... It was incredibly beautiful. The sea had a silver-grey sheen,
the clouds were ablaze, and, on top of it all, as in some kind of perfect postcard,
we saw dolphins jumping out of the water! Everything had a certain tinge,
red or gold, matt, contrasted. There is a late poem by Blaise Cendrars in which
the poet says he wants to keep for himself the sunrises he watches (naked).
I'm going to keep them all to myself, he writes.
We entered Odessa running after the sun, but we couldn't catch up with it.

—

A man called Pacha, working at the Odessa harbour,
came on board to drink our vodka.

– I went into the cosmos. (*He drinks*).
– Really?
– Yeah. I spent ten years there. It's not that exciting up there, you know.
– And when you came back, what did you do?
– I dived under water, very deep, for twenty years.
It's much better than the cosmos...
– Why? (*He drinks.*)
– More difficult, more dangerous, and there are fish.
– Twenty years, that's a long time!
– We were looking for Atlantis, it was not easy... (*He drinks.*)
– Did you find it?
– Yes. (*He drinks.*) But that was not very interesting either.
In fact, the cosmos and Atlantis are made for those with no imagination.
The real paradise is here. Where it is cosmic and aquatic. It's where one flies and dives. (*He drinks.*) It took me thirty years to understand that witticism, I'm that stupid. Now I know: the real conquest is the people, the encounters, there, on earth... (*He drinks.*)
– Do you drink to celebrate that discovery?
– No, I drink out of a sense of weather.
– Ha? (*He drinks*)
It's forty degrees in Odessa, so my blood must be forty degrees too.
– Hence the vodka.
– Exactly. With wine I would be below the required temperature, with brandy I would be over... (*He finishes the bottle.*)

—

(*Dialogue heard in Odessa's Museum of Literature, under the reproduction of Nicolas V. Gogol's portrait by Alexander Ivanov, during Soundwalk's 'Syndrome of Ulysses' concert.*)
– Does Nicolas Vassilievitch Gogol appreciate this music?
– If he smiles, it means he must like it...
– You don't know that Gogol always laughs and cries at the same time!
– He has a very big nose.

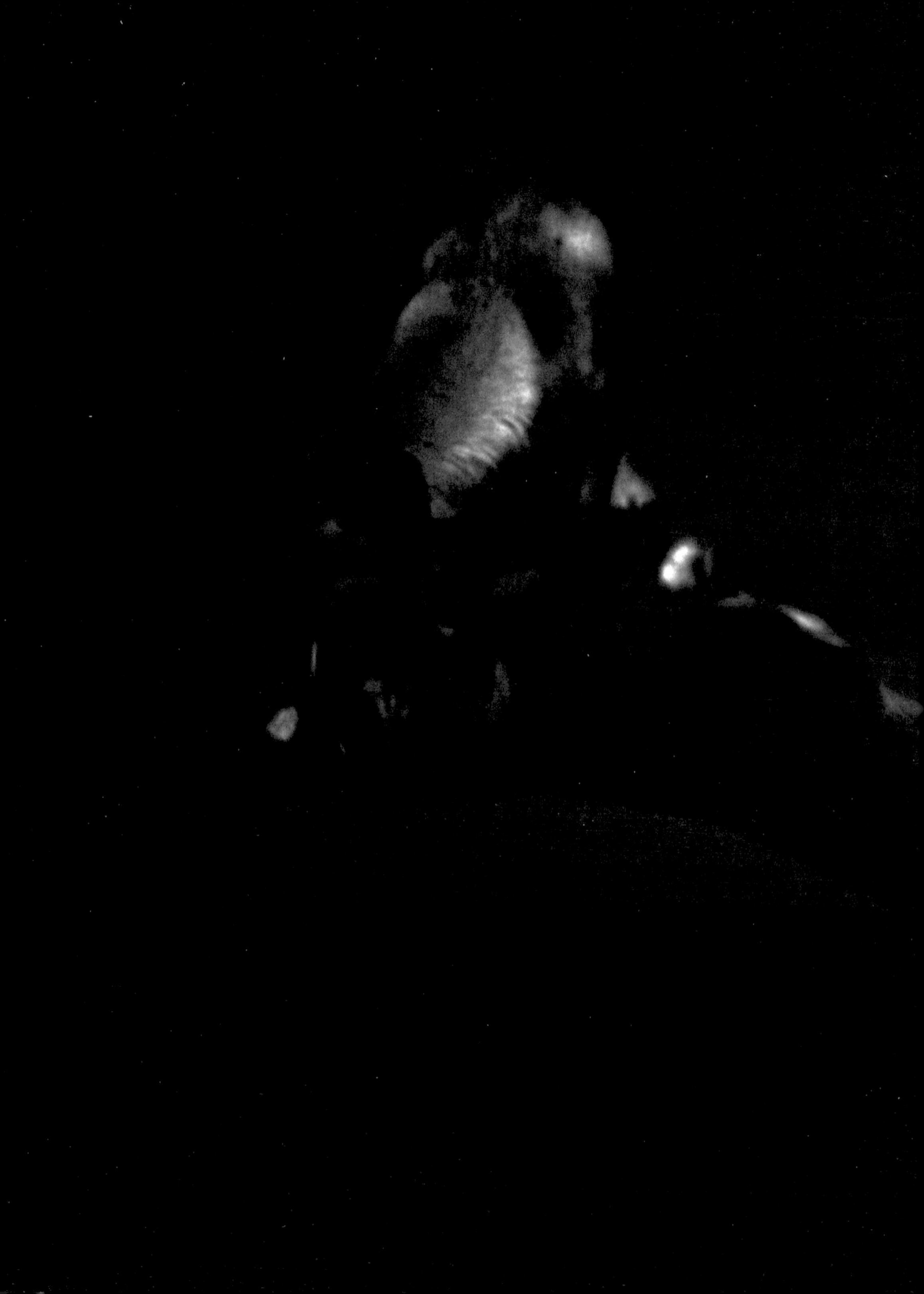

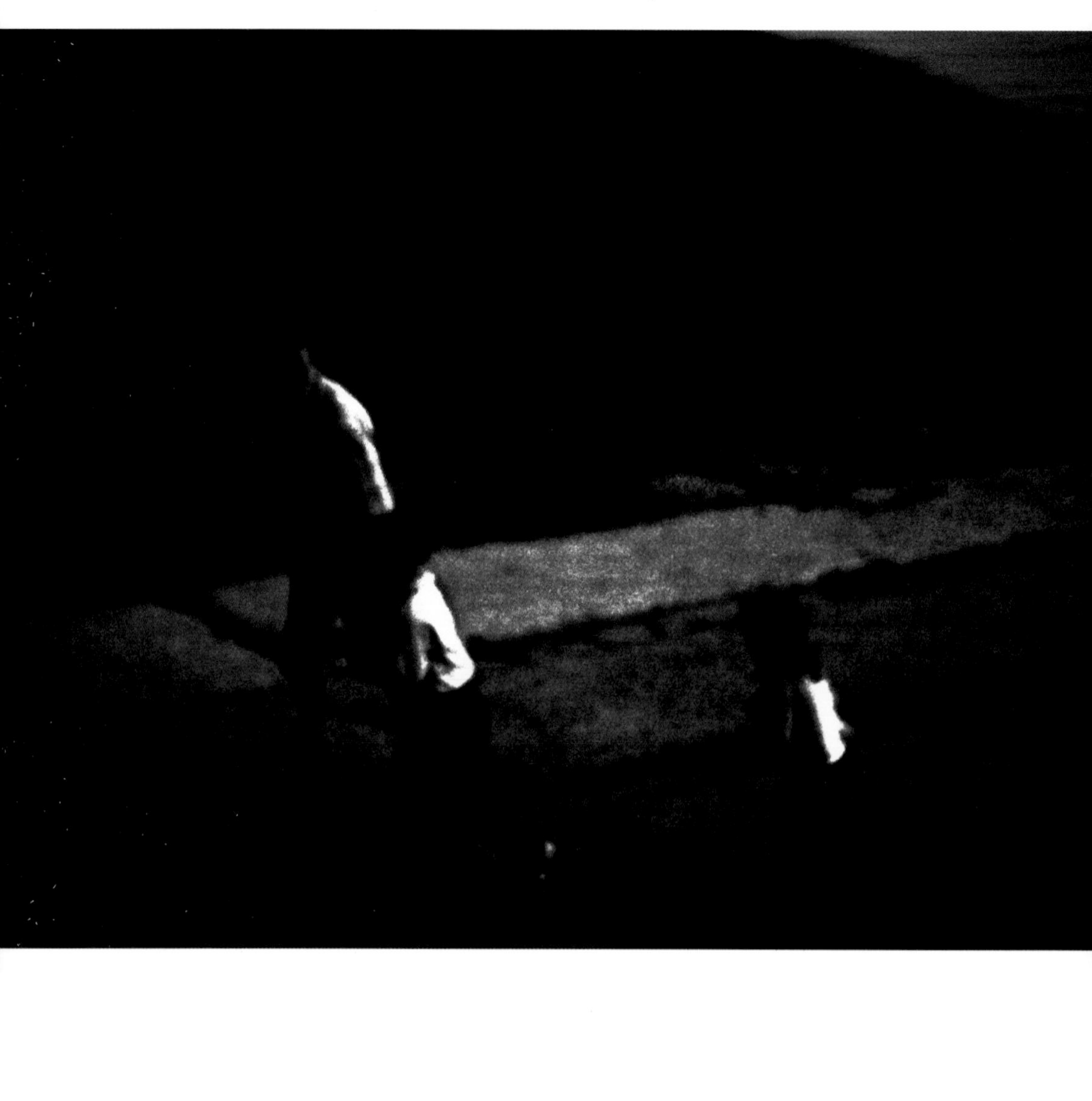

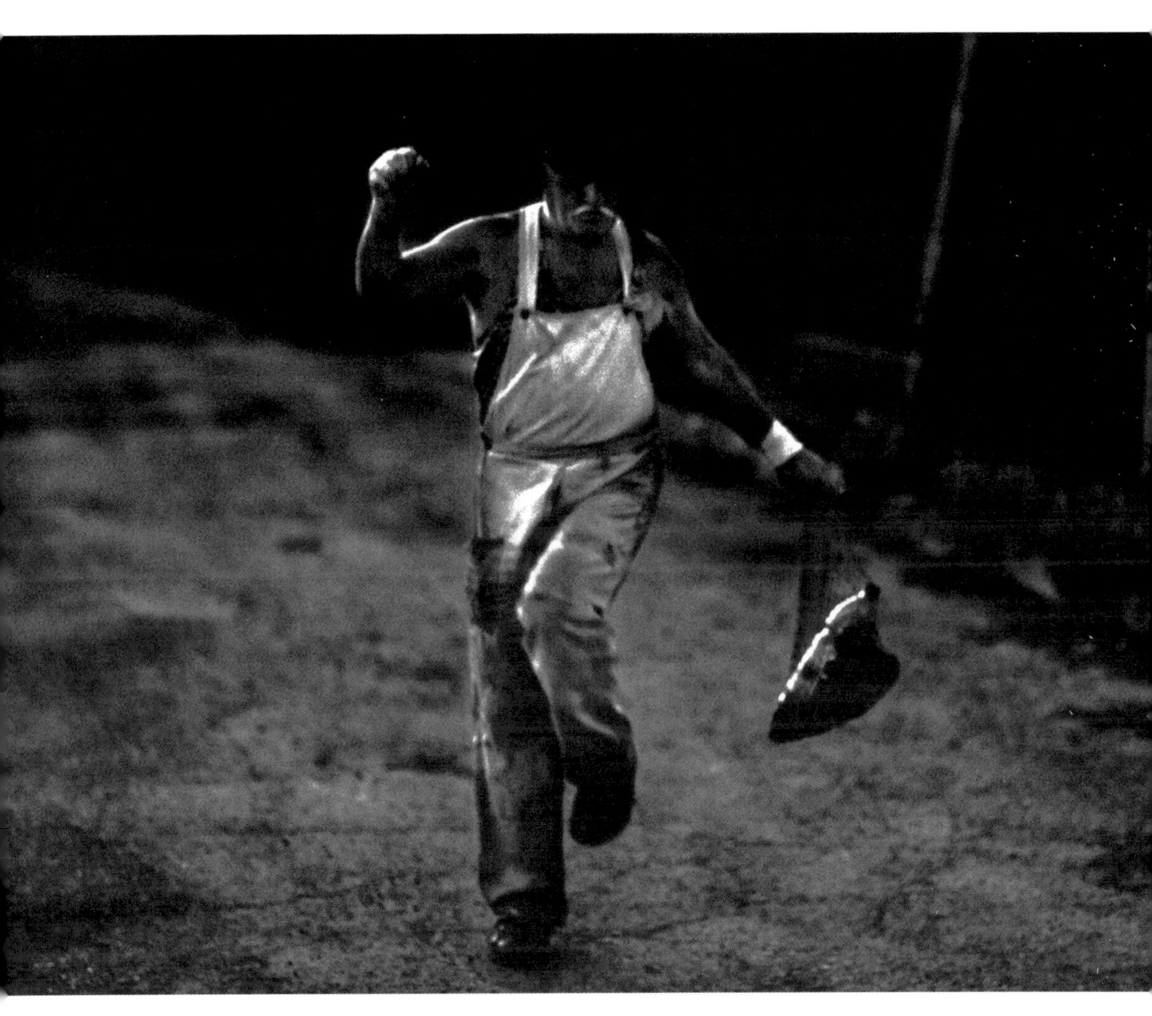

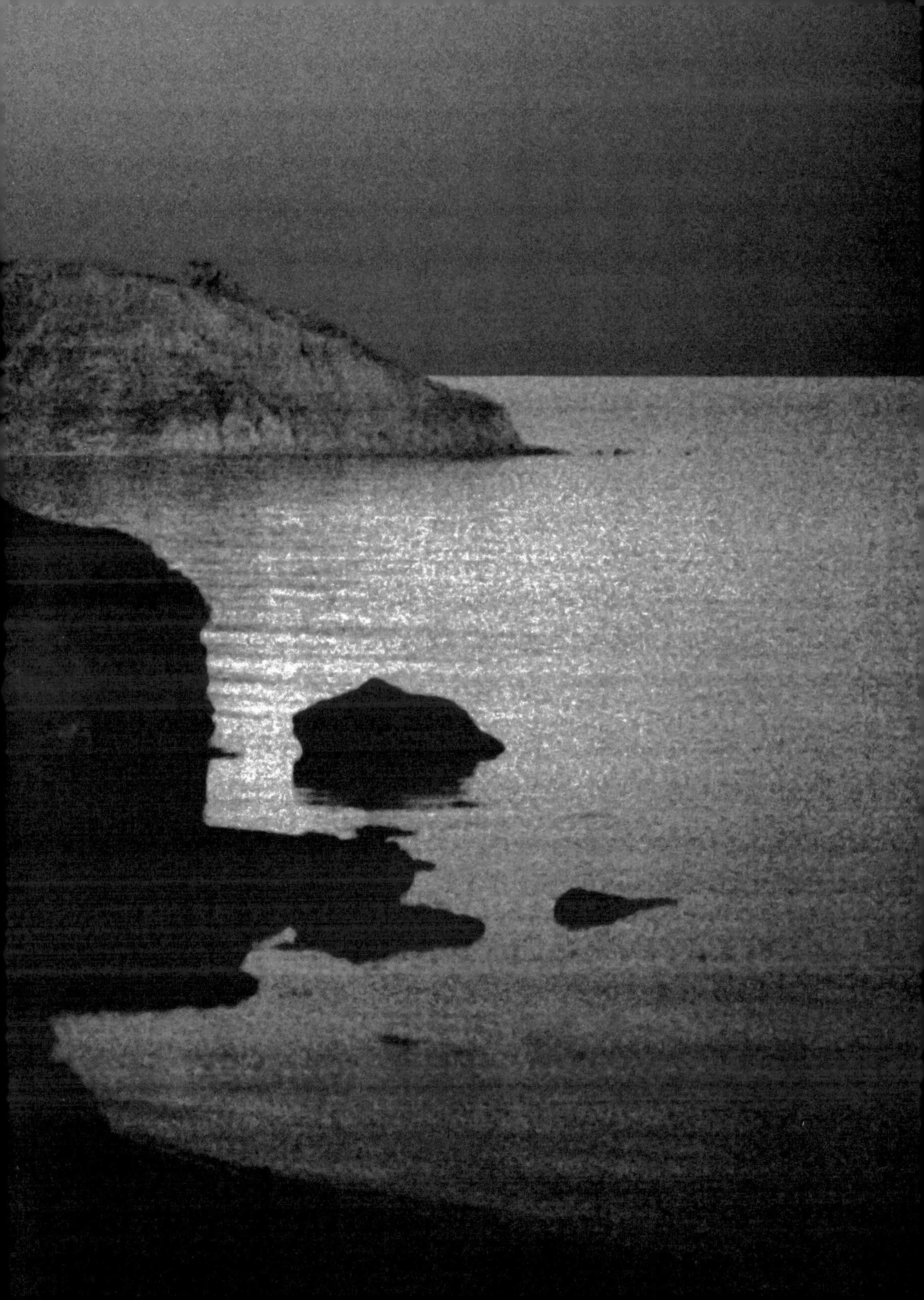

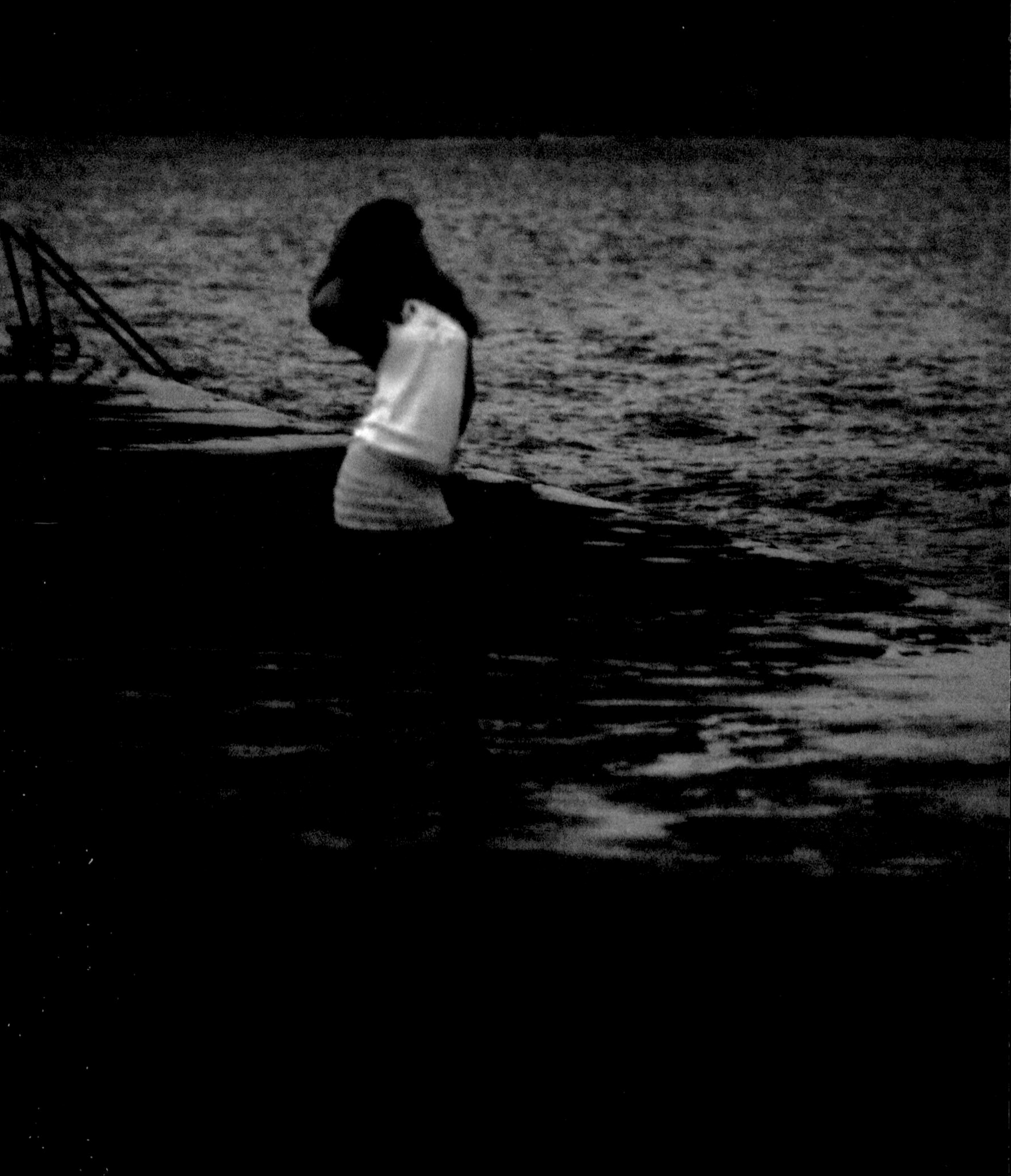

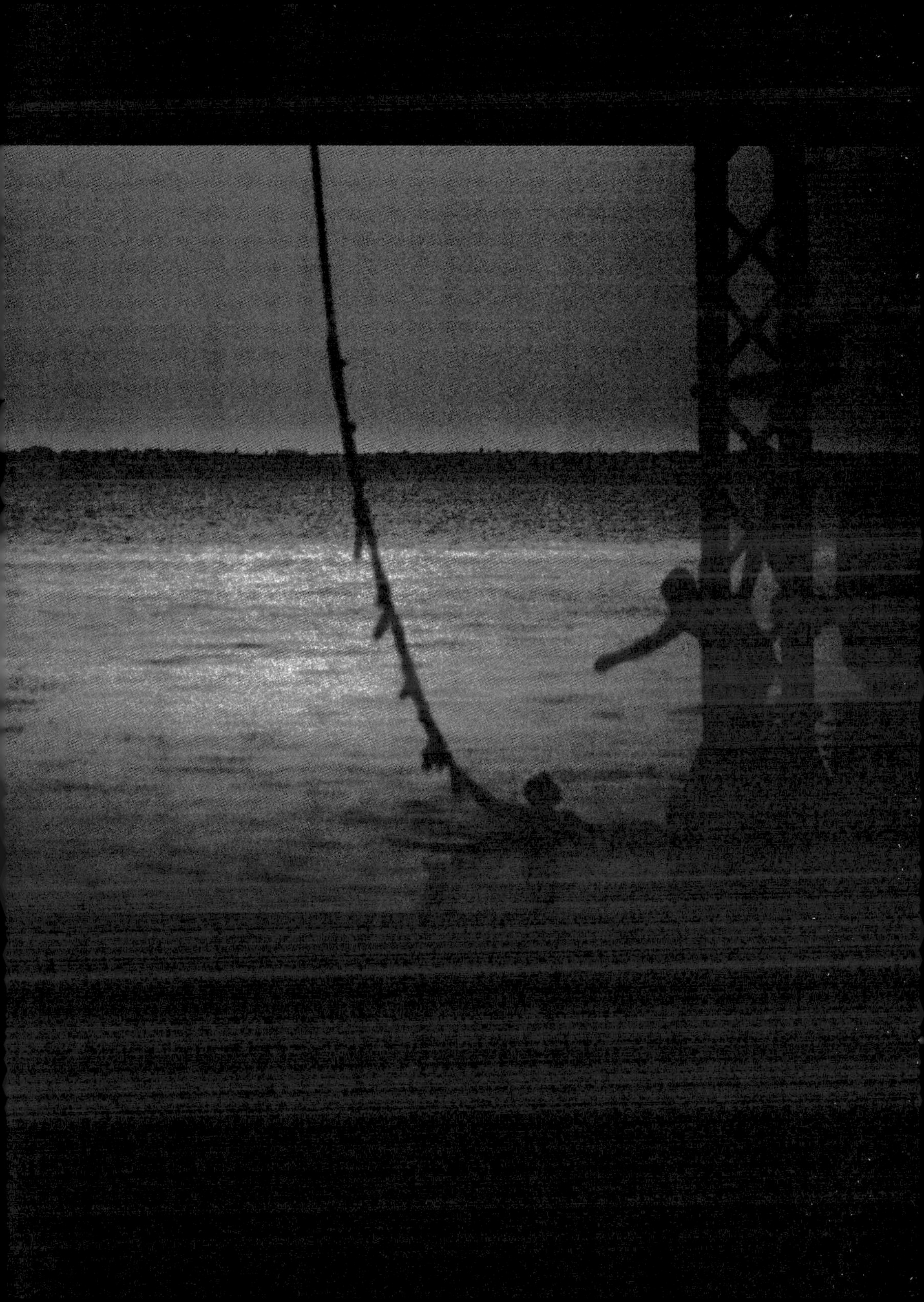

– What about you, do you like it?

– Yes.

– And Mila?

– Who is Mila?

– The one who looks like a child and wears a pink dress.

– She surely must sleep in a fridge to keep such a youthful complexion at her age!

– Does she like it?

She says it's music to make love to slowly…

—

Ania has come to sing for us, she played hesitant arpeggios on our Turkish guitar, as if to emphasize the primacy of heart over Art. Her voice was soaring, ascending, whistling. A charm. A charm who had drunk a big glass of vodka before recording, and had left us the words of her songs, scrawling them in red ink.

И дальние моря кричят ему "Ура".

—

Odessis a city that sleeps. We invent underground lives in its ruined palaces, naps on the balconies whose windows are covered in flyspecks, overrun with wisteria, wobbly beneath the weight of snow, in which an old edition of books by Mayakovski and Pushkin would rot at our feet, between a bowl of milk for the cat, ashtrays full and wet, holy pictures with children's mottos written in ancient alphabets. Life would pass sweetly, almost poisoned, slow, exhausted by dreams. It is characteristic of the forgotten large Slavic cities – St. Petersburg, Sebastopol, Yalta – to resolutely take chimera for glories, intentions for acts. They hold the secret of a certain intoxication, a certain decomposition that makes you more smoke than flesh, more dreams than actions. Cities for cats and daydreaming.

– Definition of Oblomovism: to ask What's the point… and fall back to sleep.
– Arthur, what about the Journal? And why are you asleep?
– I'm not asleep, I'm creating. These things are slow like snails.
One must sometimes wait and just look at the ceiling.
A very attractive opera singer has come to recite some Mandelstam and Pushkin.
I questioned Stephan on the methods of recording.
– Why does she have to whisper into the microphone?
Tiny voices are more moving. They are almost forgotten already?

–

Back to the sea. (E30 44'98.7)) I saw a white butterfly twelve miles from the coasts. Do marine butterflies exist? The presence of such an insect would presuppose a caterpillar able to walk on water and feed on salt.
To walk on water must be exhausting, and salt must burn one's throat.
It is quite improbable that a living organism puts up with such an austere life.
Anyway, the problem of the chrysalis remains, for what could it hang on in order to transform? On the whitecap of a wave? Under the fin of a fish?
Or else it has the capacity to float, and therefore it would let itself be carried by the tide like a cork. Hence its white colour for, not being able to fix colours because of the eddy of the sea, the marine butterfly would chose a non-colour: white.
It could have chosen black, but I assume it has a joyful and serene disposition.
The marine butterfly is therefore white.

We were sailing in the open sea for six hours with waves at our back, they pushed us gently and we went with them, and the boat was not pitching, and it was all good. I was daydreaming on the theme of the marine butterfly.

Saint-Georges E29 34'46.2

Conversation between Stephan and myself as the sun sets in the Danube delta, in Rumania. The swamps were becoming silver white and the sky was on fire, the birds were racing with us, flying at water level. There were ibis, herons and many other birds whose names I don't know. Stephan has a bizarre imagination, he was starting a comparison when I interrupted him.

– It’s as beautiful as…
– A naked woman?
– As beautiful as buried wrecks, as cabins of ghost planes eaten by rust,
as that windmill from Ceaucescu’s time that I would like to photograph:
a wooden and iron turbine that has never turned. A nothing mill.
– You are gloomy! Where are we going?
– To Periplava.
In Saint George, an old fisherman was chanting poems while playing electric guitar.
His studio was filled with speakers, he was deaf, and was crying
his lost love in Russian: Ой мама!… Ой мама!… но есть любовь на свете…

—

Periplava E29 33’71.7

– We’ll be in Periplava at ten and Kalinka will be waiting for you.
– What’s that, Kalinka?
– Six women and two little girls who sing in unison
the songs of the Danube delta.
They welcomed us in a school, served us bad tepid coffee.
There were hens with feathers on their claws, a stove in tinplate,
an Orthodox cross on each wall, portraits of Romanian kings
and revolutionaries with four guns hanging from their belt.
– Our songs are in Russian…
– Opposite our village, there’s Ukraine…
– Just there, on the other bank?
– Yes. Five minutes in a boat, but we never go there.
– The name of our village actually means “crossing”.
– One can see the golden onions of the Ukrainian churches…
– My father is buried there. To bring him flowers, I must have a visa.
– Reason for visiting Ukraine: flowers on my father’s grave!

Galati E28 01’57.9

Radio waves travel in a nebula called Ether.
On the sea, they are stronger and freer, in their element,
for nothing obstructs their journey, no wall, no tree,
and that’s why we all acted as sailors.

—

Constantza N42 03’64.8

Stephan and I have heard that Maria Dragomiroiu was the greatest diva in Romania. For phonetic reasons, we simply called her Maria. We met her after a concert, she was given roses and, one by one, the girls from the audience came to pose with her. They told Maria she was very beautiful and she thanked them. One doesn’t talk to Maria Dragomiroiu without telling her she is very beautiful.
– Maria, you are very beautiful but we cannot record in your dressing room, the outside noise comes in through the gaps in the doors, it would spoil your magnificent voice...
– Thank you. We will go in my car. My car, quickly! Chauffeur! Chauffeur!
It was the car of an Arab sheikh, where everything was electric and flashy.
She made us choose a song by playing her records one by one, singing over them to make sure we understood it was her singing.
She gave us five autographs and two records. “For your mothers.”
Maria Dragomiroiu loves Maria Dragomiroiu with a passion. She is a diva who has become more beautiful in her own eyes than her dream, and who admires herself.

—

Mamaia N43 03’64.8

(Conversation with Titinia.)
– Stephan, you’re a musician?

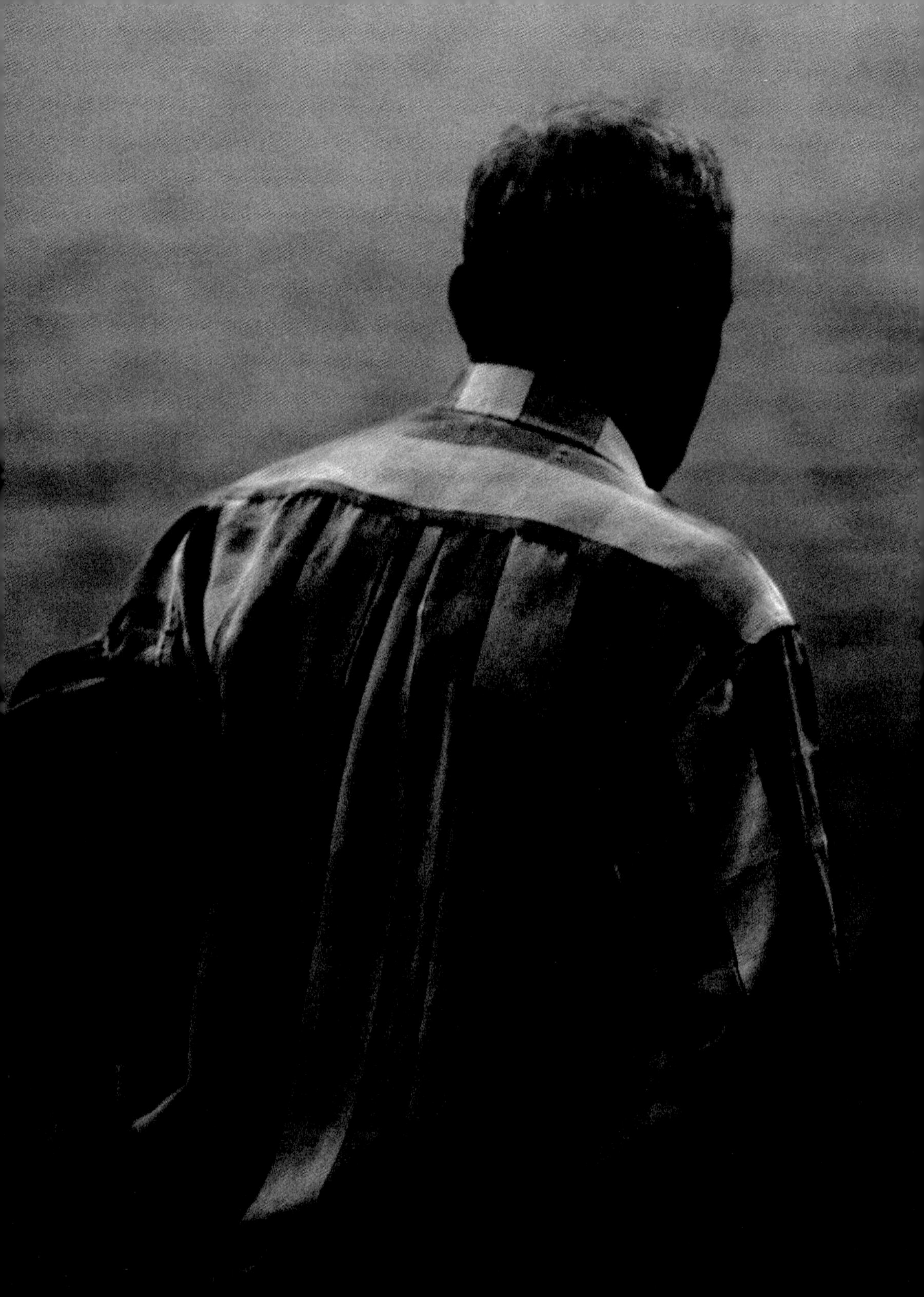

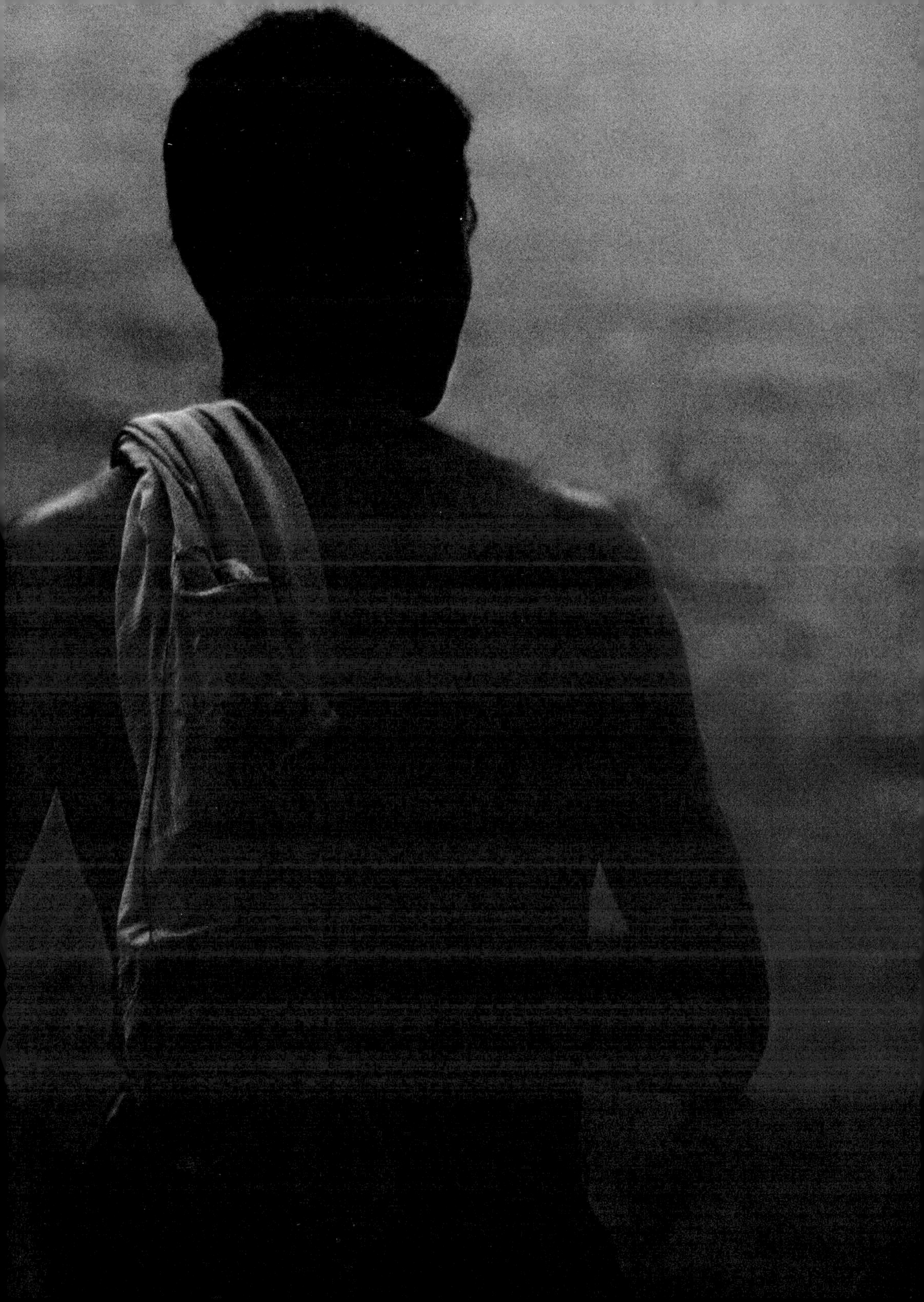

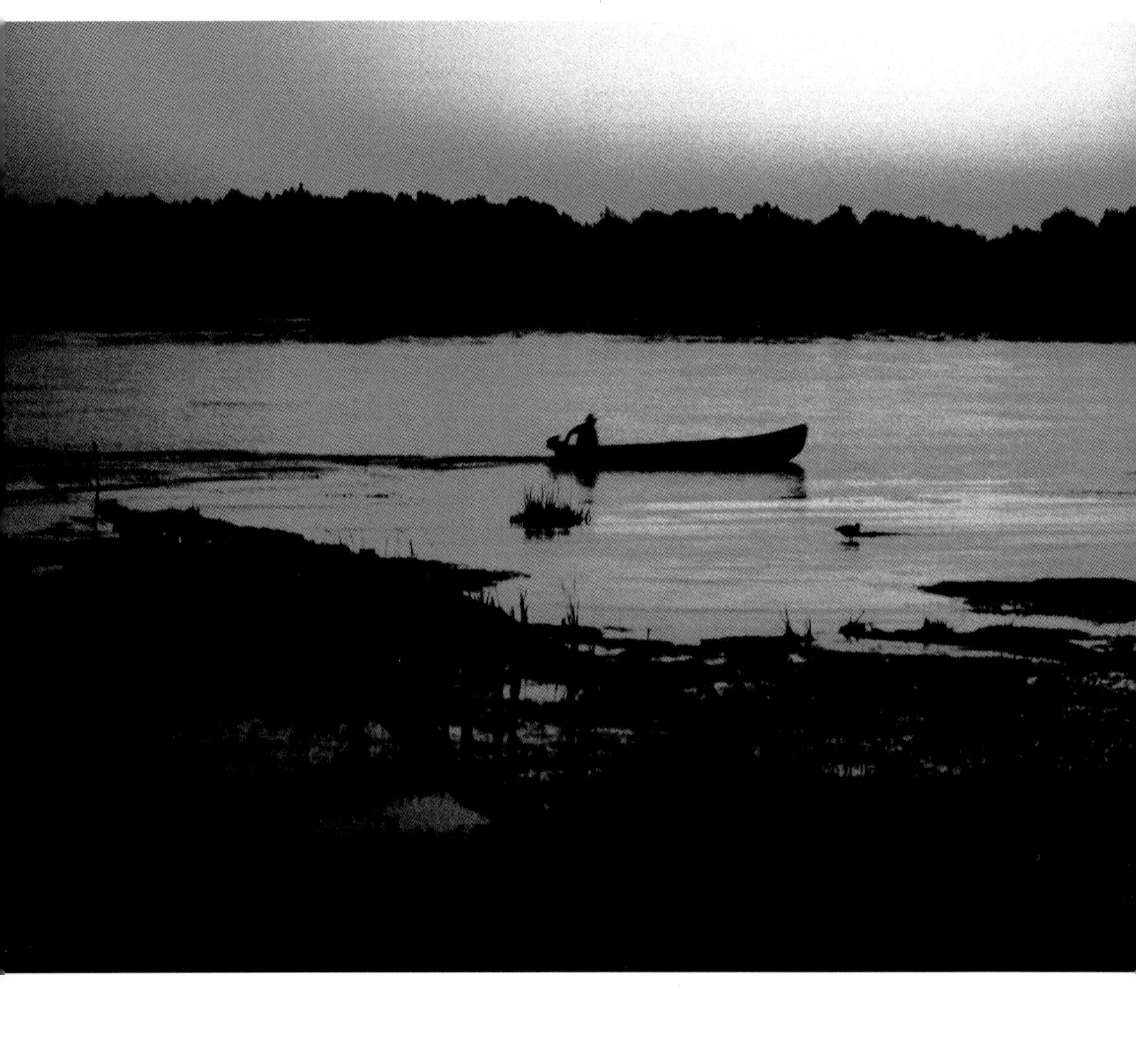

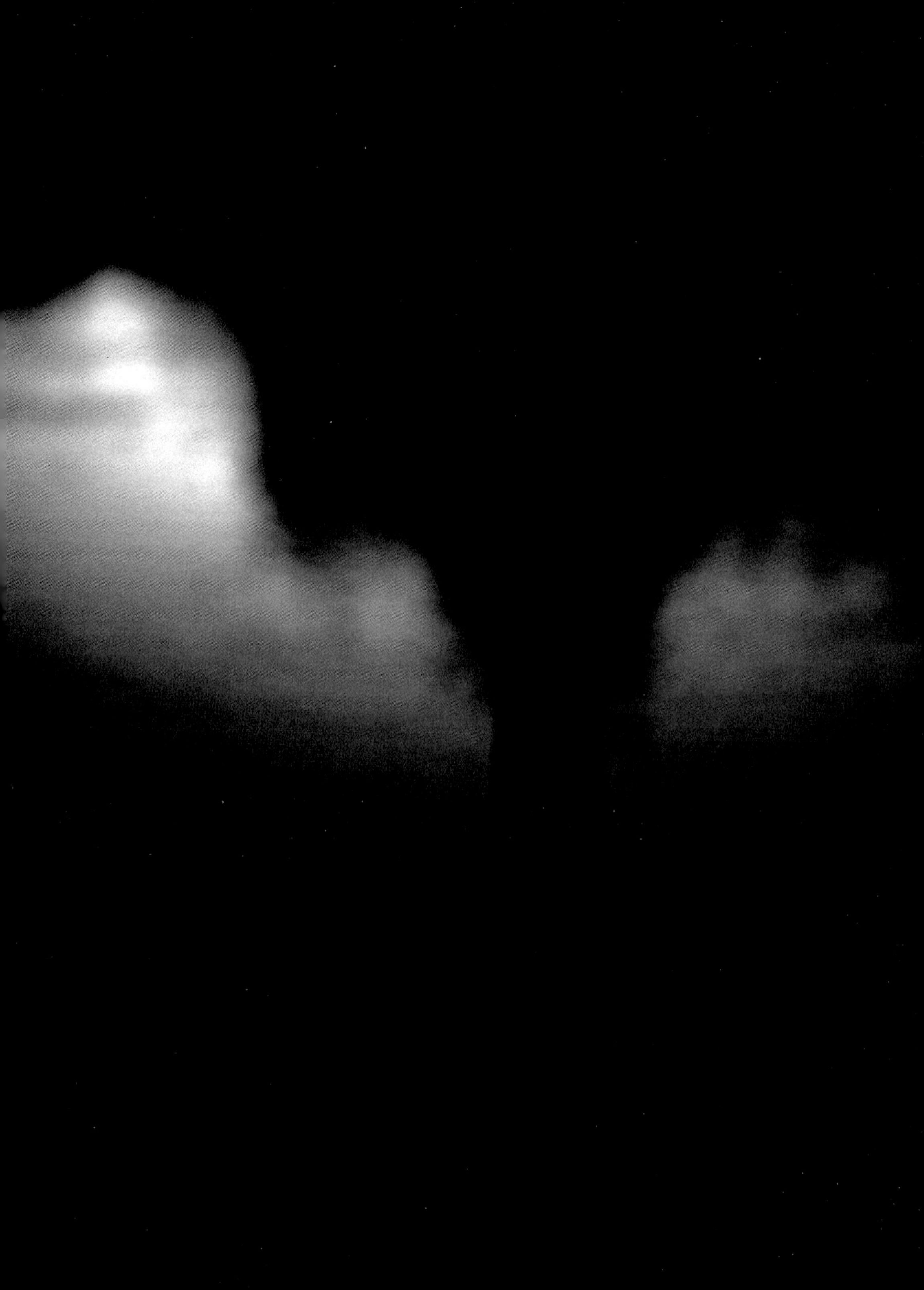

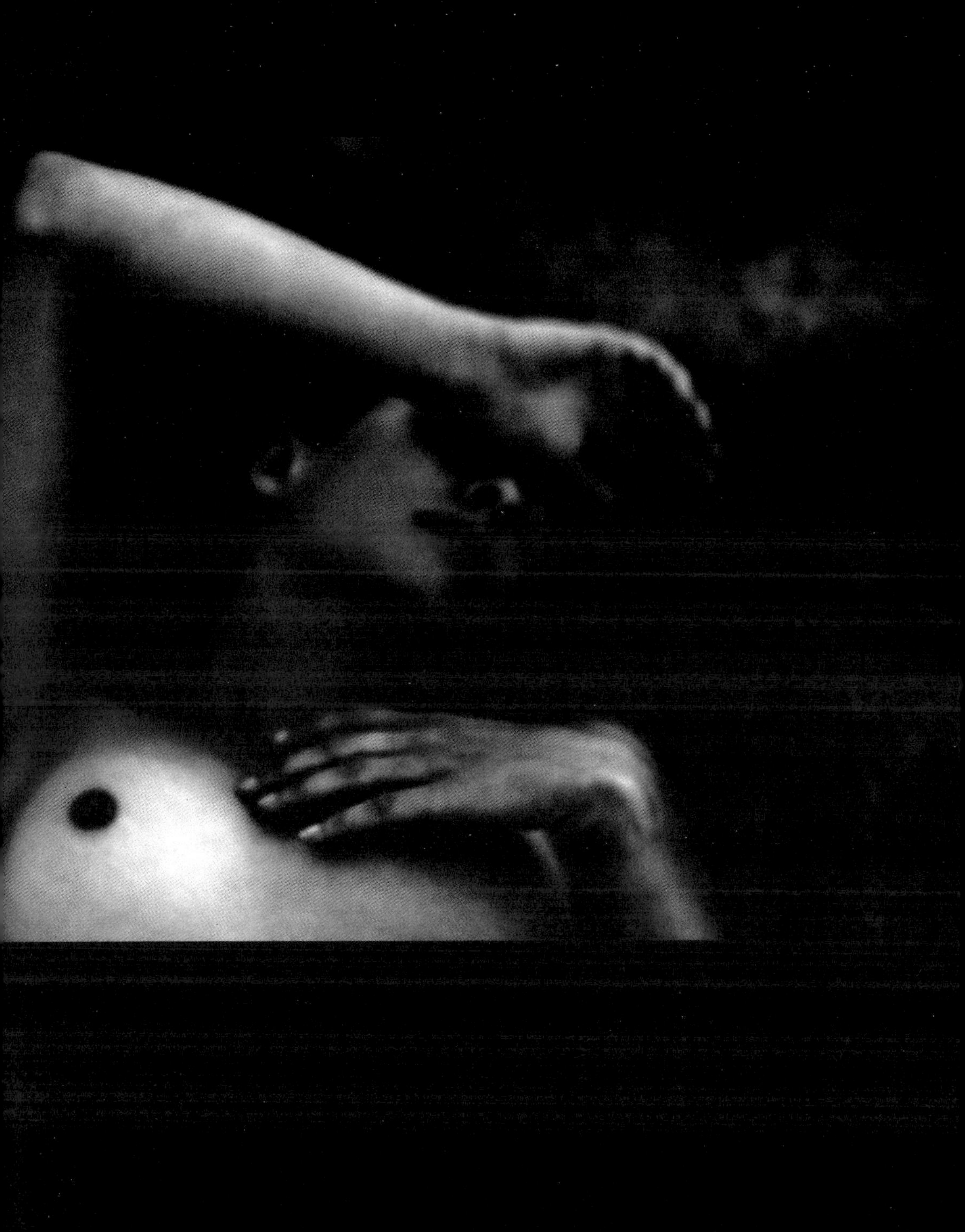

– Not exactly, because I play with the music and the voices of others…
– Arthur, you're a writer?
– Certainly not. I have only books and no publishers…
– Are you famous?
– Across the whole of the Black Sea!
– Are you leaving today?
– Yes, we are leaving now for Bulgaria.
– We have to see the Turkish border to loop our loop.
– And after, you're going back home?
– We don't know yet…
– Titinia?
– Yes?
– Can we call you Medea?

—

Burgas E27 58'61.6

Mr Yourdanov is a Bulgarian poet. He wears old American rock band T-shirts
and considers old age a second youth. He was sitting among six women,
as befits a poet. He was eating the tarama he had prepared,
the cheesecake one of the women had baked him and whose ingredients
(eggs, Bulgarian yoghurt, cheese) he had mixed. He was drinking whisky, and
the women were smoking while complimenting him on his poetry. In his garden,
there were family photos hanging on the walls, they were spending
the summer outside. There were also birds' statues, among them a stork
with red stilts, paper waterlilies, garlic still purple, seashells woven in a fishing net.
Mr Yourdanov has met the whole world, he sang with Vysotsky and shook hands
with the pope. His house is like his poet's head: full of disparate images.
One should grow old like Mr Yourdanov, in a three-storey house on the seafront,
where not one centimetre of wall is bare,
where one would spend one's old age like a child looks at its marbles,
where one would dream in the company of storks and women.

And when it's time to go, one would say, smiling: "Already?"
Mr. Yourdanov read three of his poems with the indolent voice of a child who has everything he wishes.

Sinemorets E27 58'61.6

We went right to the top of the Strandzha mountains to a dance.
We left in a red and white van with a traditional orchestra.
They had a bass drum that one beats with a needle and a mace,
a flute without a mouthpiece, a goat's skin in which were planted three tubas,
an accordion, and two singers.
They knew a song for each river in the country, and sang each time
we crossed a bridge. The last recording was done in a village hall,
under a boar's head. In the church, each dead one had donated an icon, and
it resulted in hundreds and hundreds of images piled on the ground, eaten by mice
and time. We were offered home made schnapps: a yellow and almost opaque liquid
that burnt the liver and smelt of dandelions. We had seven countries to drink to,
and how many regions? The mountains began to move like waves,
and melt into one another like clouds. Stephan and I were drunk,
on a flat rock above the empty space.
– Look at that! It looks like the storm off the coast of Russia...
– I want to smoke a whole handful of tobacco from Istanbul's Grand Bazaar!
– Your beard is made of this tobacco! Hold on, take that box. Give me the schnapps.
– That's because since Batumi, I haven't found any barber...
– One doesn't play with one's beard passed Georgia. Because Slavs have no hair...
– And Romanians make tripe soup!
– Is Moldavia on the Black Sea?
– Almost! No... give me the schnapps.
– How many Medeas did we meet?
– Each time the word "beauty" was pronounced. We had...
– The sun is rising! It's the end...

It's the last time Medea bewitched us.

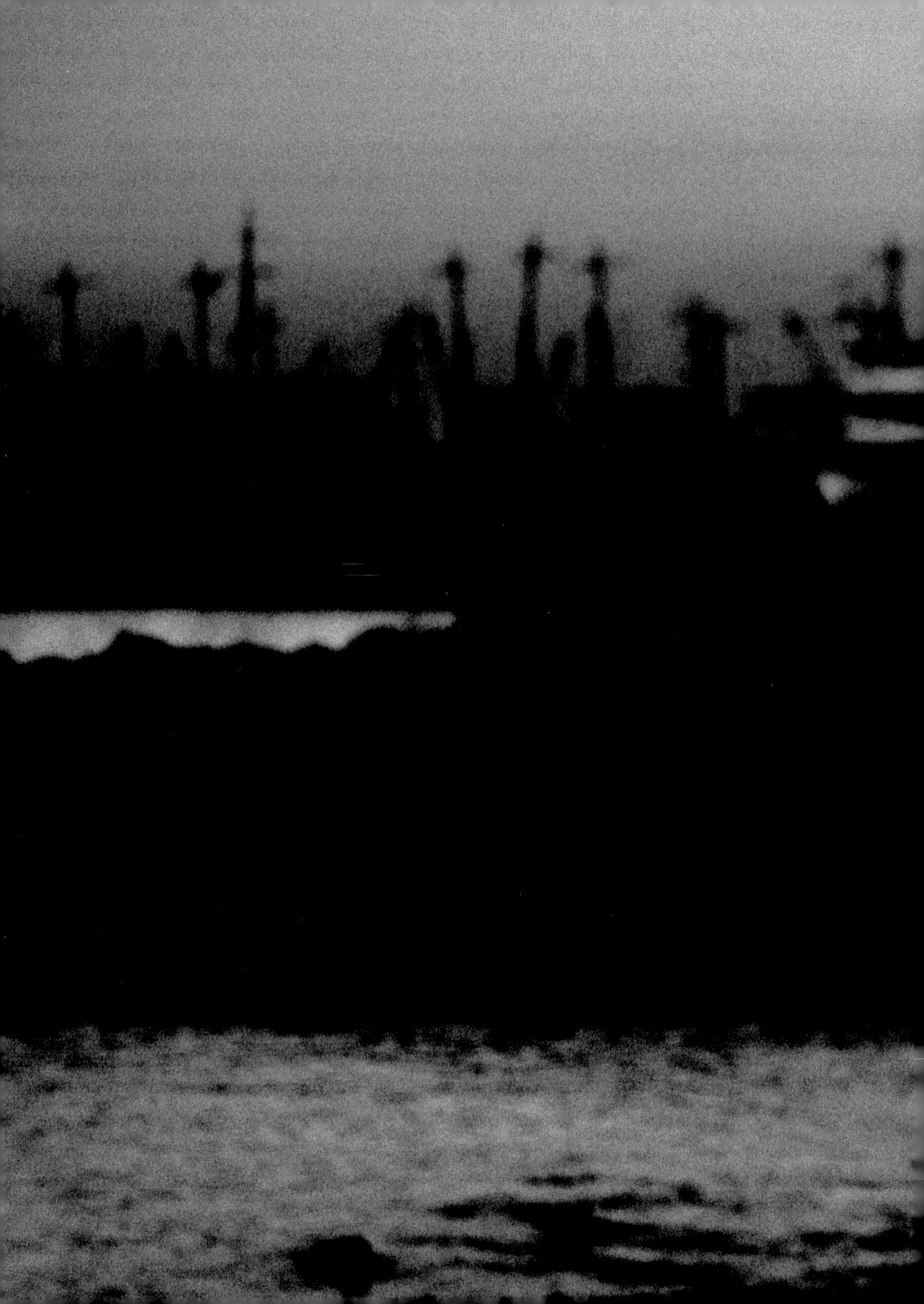

Epilogue—Zabernovo E27 33'66

It would finish thus on that day. It was in the air and it was in things, nothing that could be ignored, nothing to do either, a horrible fatality. The calendar is a code with strict and numbered rules, one does not negotiate with it. The Mayas had conceived a very complex and very beautiful one that instructed people in what they had to think each day. There has never been a 32nd July, or a 32nd August... It was the fixed day, we had to leave. We left the boat backwards, our luggage piled up high in the annexe, like a mountain of lego. Kamran went to take down the spider-aerial he had fixed on top of the mast.

I was mistaken about that aerial: when one holds it in one's hand, is looks more like the pappus of a dandelion than a spider.

All our equipment was switched off, the scanners rolled up in cloth to counter the jolts, they will travel back to New York by plane.

Who said: "*To leave is to die a little...*"?

And to go back, is it to die for good?

Acknowledgments

Deniz Alnitemiz, Meme Avaloneli, Annie Bri, Maria Cucu, Skatri Olva, Lily Standefer, Nedyalko Yourdanov, for their artistic contributions.

Captain Cagdas Varliklioglu, Caner Demir, Mustapha Yilmaz, Chef Hassan,"The Vicomtesse" Crew.

Special thanks

Laurence Cornet, Fabrice Desprez, Альянс Франсез / the French Institute Alliance Francaise in Odessa, Jean-Yves Leloup, Yury Marychev, Yulia Mochalova, Vincent Moon, Anna Olekhnovych, Emma Reeves, Mikheil Saakachvili - Président de Géorgie, Nathalie de Saint-Phalle, Giorgi Samkharadze, Romain Servat, Lily Standefer

and also

Angela Baciu, Nastya Belan, Levan Berulava, Elina Boncheva, Bertrand Bouard, Valeri Chekheria, Tania Crasnianski, Sergey Demidov, Sonia Desprez, Deniz Erol, Sophian Fanen, Sasha Fe, Julia Govor, Matthew Hoag, Ekaterina Kibovskaya, Yuri Koval'ov, Daria Likhovitskaya, the Literature Museum in Odessa, Dr. Lauren Ninoshvili, Arkady Petrov, Bianca Rusu, Geraldine Sarratia, Zeynep Sicimoglu, Katya Smolina, Jennie Sobol, Alexandra Tzvetkova

Printed by
Petro Ofsetas
Lituanie
EUROPE
April 2012